PERGAMON INTERNATIONAL LIBRARY
of Science, Technology, Engineering and Social Studies
The 1000-volume original paperback library in aid of education,
industrial training and the enjoyment of leisure
Publisher: Robert Maxwell, M.C.

PITFALLS IN HUMAN RESEARCH
Ten Pivotal Points

(PGPS-67)

_____ Publisher's Notice to Educators _____

THE PERGAMON TEXTBOOK
INSPECTION COPY SERVICE

An inspection copy of any book published in the Pergamon
International Library will gladly be sent without obligation for
consideration for course adoption or recommendation. Copies may
be retained for a period of 60 days from receipt and returned if not
suitable. When a particular title is adopted or recommended for
adoption for class use and the recommendation results in a sale of
12 or more copies, the inspection copy may be retained with our
compliments. If after examination the lecturer decides that the
book is not suitable for adoption but would like to retain it for his
personal library, then our Educators' Discount of 10% is allowed on
the invoiced price. The Publishers will be pleased to receive
suggestions for revised editions and new titles to be published in this
important International Library.

PERGAMON GENERAL PSYCHOLOGY SERIES

Editor: Arnold P. Goldstein, *Syracuse University*
Leonard Krasner, *SUNY, Stony Brook*

TITLES IN THE PERGAMON GENERAL PSYCHOLOGY SERIES
(Added Titles in Back of Volume)

The terms of our inspection copy service apply to all the above books. A complete catalogue of all books in the Pergamon International Library is available on request.

The Publisher will be pleased to receive suggestions for revised editions and new titles.

ii

PITFALLS IN HUMAN RESEARCH
Ten Pivotal Points

Theodore Xenophon Barber
Medfield Foundation, Medfield, Massachusetts

M.D., Ph.D.
1977

PERGAMON PRESS INC
New York / Toronto / Oxford / Sydney / Frankfurt / Paris

Pergamon Press Offices:

U.S.A.	Pergamon Press Inc., Maxwell House, Fairview Park, Elmsford, New York 10523, U.S.A.
U.K.	Pergamon Press Ltd., Headington Hill Hall, Oxford OX3, OBW, England
CANADA	Pergamon of Canada, Ltd., 207 Queen's Quay West, Toronto 1, Canada
AUSTRALIA	Pergamon Press (Aust) Pty. Ltd., 19a Boundary Street, Rushcutters Bay, N.S.W. 2011, Australia
FRANCE	Pergamon Press SARL, 24 rue des Ecoles, 75240 Paris, Cedex 05, France
WEST GERMANY	Pergamon Press GmbH, 6242 Kronberg/Taunus, Frankfurt-am-Main, West Germany

Copyright © 1976 Pergamon Press Inc.

Library of Congress Cataloging in Publication Data

Barber, Theodore Xenophon, 1927 -
    Pitfalls in human research.

    (Pergamon general psychology series)
    Bibliography: p.
    Includes indexes.
    1. Psychological research. I. Title. [DNLM:
1. Behavioral sciences. 2. Research. BF76.5 B234p]
BF76.5.B37   1976   150'.7'2   76-13488
ISBN 0-08-020935-1

Printed in the United States of America

Contents

The Author

Theodore X. Barber (Ph.D., American University) is Director of Research at the Medfield Foundation and State Hospital in Medfield, Massachusetts. He is widely recognized as a leading researcher in the area of hypnosis and has published 150 scientific papers on hypnosis and other topics (such as biofeedback, the psychology of pain, and pitfalls in research). He has also authored six previous books (*Hypnosis: A Scientific Approach; LSD, Marihuana, Yoga and Hypnosis; Biofeedback and Self-Control; Hypnotic Phenomena; Hypnosis, Imagination, and Human Potentialities;* and *Advances in Altered States of Consciousness and Human Potentialities*). He has served as President of the Massachusetts Psychological Association and of the Hypnosis Division of the American Psychological Association and has served on the editorial boards of *Journal of Abnormal Psychology, Behavior Therapy, American Journal of Community Psychology*, and *Biofeedback and Self-Regulation*.

Introduction

Since experiments are designed and carried out by fallible individuals, they have as many pitfalls as other human endeavors. In this text we shall discuss ten pivotal points in research where investigators and experimenters can go astray. By becoming sensitized to these pitfalls, those of us who are engaged in experimental research may be better able to avoid them in our own studies. Also, those of us who utilize research results in our teaching or practice may be able to use experimental studies more wisely if we are sensitized to the many possibilities they contain for misleading results and conclusions.

Two questions will be at the forefront of discussion: 1) At what pivotal points in the complex research process can the experimental study go astray and give rise to misleading results and conclusions? 2) What steps can researchers take to avoid these pitfalls? To answer these questions, I shall first focus on those aspects of experimental studies that are under the control of the investigator and then on those aspects that are under the control of the experimenter. I shall begin by making a distinction between the investigator and the experimenter.

Although the investigator and the experimenter can be the same person, their roles are functionally quite different, and it is rather common in recent research to find one person in the role of investigator and another person in the role of experimenter.

The *investigator* decides that a study is to be conducted, how it is to be designed and carried out, and how it is to be analyzed and interpreted. Thus, the investigator is responsible for the experimental design, the procurement and training of experimenters, the overall conduct of the study, the analysis of the results, the interpretation of data, and the writing of the final research report.

The *experimenter*, on the other hand, is the person who conducts the study—who tests the subjects, administers the experimental procedures, and observes and records the subjects' responses. Thus, strictly speaking a person in the role of the experimenter is responsible for the collection of the data but is not responsible for the experimental design, the analysis, and interpretation of the data, or the final research report.

In brief, even though the same person may take the role of both an investigator and an experimenter, these two roles are functionally quite different. Furthermore, in much present-day research, investigators are typically highly paid professionals whereas experimenters are often graduate or undergraduate students.[1]

Table 1 Investigator and Experimenter Effects

Investigator Effects

    I.   Investigator Paradigm Effect
    II.   Investigator Experimental Design Effect
    III. Investigator Loose Procedure Effect
    IV. Investigator Data Analysis Effect
    V.   Investigator Fudging Effect

Experimenter Effects

    VI. Experimenter Personal Attributes Effect
    VII. Experimenter Failure to Follow the Procedure Effect
    VIII. Experimenter Misrecording Effect
    IX. Experimenter Fudging Effect
    X.   Experimenter Unintentional Expectancy Effect

Table 1 lists ten major pitfalls in research that can directly or indirectly give rise to misleading results and conclusions. As shown in the top portion of Table 1, misleading results and conclusions in an experimental study can derive from the investigator's paradigm, from his experimental design, from the "looseness" of his experimental procedure, from his analysis of the data and, possibly, from his fudging of data. As shown in the bottom portion of Table 1, misleading results and conclusions can also be produced by the experimenter's personal attributes, by his failure to follow the experimental procedures, by his misrecording of data, by his fudging of data, and by his expectancies. Each of these effects will be discussed in turn.

Before I turn to the discussion of each of the ten pitfalls listed in Table 1, however, let us note an important point. During recent years, the biasing effects and misleading conclusions that are associated with experimental research have been commonly attributed to the experimenter who carries out the study rather than to the investigator who designs and has the major responsibility for the study. Recent books (Adair, 1973; Friedman, 1967; Jung, 1971; A.G. Miller, 1972; Rosenthal, 1966; Rosenthal & Rosnow, 1969) which discussed the artifacts or pitfalls in research tended to focus on the experimenter and tended to neglect the important role of the investigator. I shall attempt to redress this imbalance by focusing equally on the role of the investigator and the role of the experimenter. I hope that it will become clear to the reader that the bias that has commonly been attributed to the experimenter who runs the study is at times actually due to the investigator who has major responsibility for the study.[2]

NOTES

1. In the early 1960s, only 37 percent of 71 biologists who were interviewed by Crane (1964) reported that they collected all of their own data. I believe this trend has accelerated in both the biological and behavioral sciences and that now most investigators only rarely serve as experimenters.

2. Although this book covers ten pitfalls in behavioral science research, there are many related topics that are not discussed. These relevant problems, which are discussed in general terms in recent texts (Adair, 1973; Jung, 1971; A.G. Miller, 1972; Rosenthal & Rosnow, 1969), and which are covered in detail in the books cited below, include the following: (a) Problems of sampling bias due to the use of volunteer subjects (Rosenthal & Rosnow, 1975). (b) Problems pertaining to inter-subject communication about the experimental procedures which derive from the fact that a substantial proportion of subjects do not keep their promise "not to talk about the experiment to others" (Farrow, Farrow, Lohss, & Taub, 1975; Wuebben, Straits, & Schulman, 1974). (c) Ethical issues pertaining to lack of confidentiality and informed consent, coercion of college students to participate in psychological experiments as part of a course requirement, the use of misleading instructions or deception to influence subjects, and the application of stress to subjects (B. Barber, Lally, Makarushka, & Sullivan, 1973). (d) Problems pertaining to the researcher and the social system (science as a system of norms, the associations of scientists, the role, functions, and social status of scientists, and social factors that affect the formulation of research problems and the publication of research findings) (Sjoberg & Nett, 1968).

Pitfall I
Investigator Paradigm Effect

In Table 1 the Investigator Paradigm Effect is listed first. This effect exerts a pervasive influence on every aspect of experimental research including the results and conclusions.

Kuhn (1962, 1970) has used the term *paradigm* to refer to a conceptual framework and a body of assumptions, belief, and related methods and techniques that are shared by a large group of scientists at a particular time. For example, in astronomy we can refer to the Copernican (heliocentric) paradigm which differed markedly from and which gradually replaced the Ptolemaic (geocentric) paradigm, and in psychology we can refer to the behavioristic paradigm which included a conceptual framework and a related body of assumptions, beliefs, and methods that were shared by a large group of psychologists until recent years. Kuhn presented historical evidence that such paradigms set boundaries for "normal" scientific research. A paradigm provides an implicit framework for the scientists working in an area. The assumptions or presuppositions of the paradigm govern the choice of problems and the "correct" methods and criteria for evaluating the solution of such selected problems. By defining what is normal, accepted, and natural, the paradigm acts as a blinder. The rules or ways of approaching problems operate more or less automatically and the scientist believes he is doing the natural or obvious thing.

Kuhn also noted, however, that paradigms are useful in providing directions for scientific research; thus they permit intensive and focused investigations. Without an accepted paradigm research would be diffuse and lead to the accumulation of disorganized facts.

Once a paradigm is established, however, the function of scientific training is to produce highly competent problem-solvers who will work within the paradigm. The important point here is that the prevailing paradigm determines not only what questions are asked but also what kinds of data are considered relevant and how the data will be gathered, analyzed, interpreted, and related to theoretical concepts (Chaves, 1968; Spanos & Chaves, 1970).

TENACITY OF PARADIGMS AND RESISTANCE TO NEW DISCOVERIES

Although a new paradigm may very slowly and imperceptibly supplant a prevailing paradigm (Toulmin, 1970; Watkins, 1970), the history of science shows that scientists often hold on tenaciously to an accepted paradigm and vigorously fight off any challenges. In fact, Planck (1936, p. 97) argued that new paradigms and theories are rarely accepted by rational persuasion of their opponents; instead, the new paradigm is accepted only after the opponents die out. Kuhn (1962, 1970) has presented a series of examples demonstrating the tenacity of paradigms and these have been supplemented in recent years by writers such as B. Barber (1961), de Grazia (1966), and Koestler (1971). Let us glance at a few of the examples presented by the latter three authors.

B. Barber (1961) noted that, although science comprises a social system in which objectivity and openness to new ideas is usually greater than in other social institutions, nevertheless, discoveries or ideas that challenge the dominant paradigm are not readily accepted. As examples, he presented the following: resistance to Copernicus' heliocentric theory from astronomers who could not break with the traditional Ptolemaic paradigm which viewed the earth as motionless; resistance to Thomas Young's wave theory of light by the scientists of the 19th century who were faithful to the corpuscular paradigm; resistance to Mendel's conception of the separate inheritance of unit characteristics by biologists who adhered to the prevailing paradigm which postulated joint and total inheritance of biological characteristics; and resistance to Ampere's theory of magnetic currents by scientists who could not fit it into the prevailing Newtonian mechanical model.

A recent example of the strength of accepted paradigms and the furious reactions that they may arouse when challenged is the case of Immanual Velikovsky. Velikovsky challenged the prevailing astronomical paradigm which assumed that only those processes which are operating today in our solar system could have operated in earlier periods of man's recorded history. The dominant "uniformitarian" paradigm, which excluded sudden global catastrophes, was frontally attacked by Velikovsky who amassed historical, geological, paleontological, and archeological evidence indicating that, during historical times, the earth had been subject to catastrophes from Venus and Mars. This new paradigm aroused furious reactions from scientists who adhered to the traditional paradigm; these reactions included attempts to stop publication of Velikovsky's book (*Worlds in Collision*) and to exclude his writing from learned journals (de Grazia, 1966; Stove, 1972). Although Velikovsky's ideas are as debatable as any radically new ideas, it appears that the furious reactions were due, at least partly, to a paradigm clash (de Grazia, Juergens, & Stecchini, 1966). It is noteworthy that some of the predictions made by Velikovsky from his paradigm have been confirmed (Anonymous, 1972a; Bargmann & Motz, 1962; Stove, 1972).

Many other examples of the effects of paradigms in preventing acceptance of research findings are presented by Kuhn (1962, 1970), Koestler (1971), and others. For instance, Koestler (1971) has shown that important experiments carried out during the 1920s, which contradicted the prevailing Darwinian paradigm by supporting Lamarck's thesis of the inheritance of acquired characteristics, were viciously attacked by the scientific establishment and that no one ever tried to replicate the experiments before condemning them.

FAILING TO "SEE" EVENTS AND "SEEING" NON-EXISTENT EVENTS

Scientists at times fail to "see" events that are incongruent with the assumptions of a prevailing paradigm. An interesting example is the failure of physicists to "see" indications of the positron even though the signs were present for many years. The positron is exactly like the electron, except that it has a positive electric charge. Apparently, physicists failed to recognize the positron because they assumed that electrons were *always* negatively charged and that positive charges were *always* carried by the much heavier protons (Hanson, 1963).

Similar considerations apply to the discovery that noble gases, such as neon and argon, can combine. This finding was not made until 1962 even though any investigator could have made the observation easily, with a few hours of effort, anytime during the 40s or 50s. It appears that the discovery was not made earlier because of the strength of the traditional assumption that noble gases simply cannot combine (Abelson, 1962).

Scientists may not only miss phenomena that do not fit their assumptions, they may also "see" non-existent phenomena, such as N-rays, when the phenomena fit the prevailing assumptions. During the early years of this century, after the discovery and acceptance of X-rays, many scientists were deluded into also "seeing" N-rays (Rostand, 1960). Nearly 100 papers on N-rays were printed in a single year (1904) in the official French scientific journal *Comptes Rendues* (de Solla Price, 1961). However, in a letter to Nature in 1904, Robert W. Wood, professor of physics at John Hopkins University, showed that all of the effects attributed to N-rays were due to wishful thinking and to the immense difficulties involved in estimating by eye the brightness of faint objects. From then on, there were no more papers on N-rays.

PARADIGMS IN PSYCHOLOGY

Hearst (1967), Krantz (1971), and others (e.g., Harlow, 1969) have noted that present-day behaviorists who adhere to the Skinnerian or operant conditioning approach appear to share a common paradigm. The Skinnerians reject competing approaches to psychology, and do not cite or utilize the work of non-operant psychologists. Hearst (1967) noted that:

> To many outsiders an operant conditioner is a hardnosed experimentalist who spends endless hours in the enthusiastic analysis of cumulative records from one or two subjects, attacks anything that sounds even mildly theoretical or physiological, ridicules anyone who has ever used statistics of the R.A. Fisher variety and ignores the work of any psychologist who does not publish in the *Journal of the Experimental Analysis of Behavior*. Not since J.B. Watson's time has any band of behaviorists seemed so assertive in its likes and dislikes and so convinced that its techniques and experimental approach will not only change psychology but in the process reshape the world. (p. 402)

In recent years, however, a "cognitive" paradigm has begun to compete with the behavioristic paradigm for the allegiance of experimental psychologists. As Katahn and Koplin (1968) pointed out, the behavioristic paradigm emphasizes objective descriptions of environmental events, operational definitions, and controlled experiments while the cognitive paradigm emphasizes internal information processing and programming. The investigator who adheres to the behavioristic paradigm seeks antecedent environmental and situational events that can be related to denotable behaviors. On the other hand, the investigator who adheres to the cognitive paradigm seeks to construct a model of internal processes and structures that can lead to the observed output. These contrasting paradigms lead to different questions and to different ways of designing and conducting investigations. Furthermore, even if psychologists who adhere to these divergent paradigms obtain similar data—which is highly unlikely since they will conduct quite different studies—their paradigms will lead to divergent interpretations of the data (Katahn & Koplin, 1968). Similarly, investigators who adhere to a third paradigm that is found in present-day psychology—the Freudian paradigm—will ask another set of questions (for example, questions pertaining to unconscious processes), will gather data in a different way (for example, by inferring unconscious processes from the words and actions of clinical patients), and will relate the data to a different frame of reference (the theoretical concepts that are derived from Freud).

Each of the prevailing paradigms in psychology determine what "facts" are to be gathered and how they are to be interpreted. Kessel (1969) noted, with regard to the behavioristic paradigm, that "the behaviorist's presuppositions have led to a choice of phenomena and methods that render his position basically irrefutable: It is hardly likely that the human being will reveal 'higher-order' [mental] activities when his eye blink or knee jerk are being conditioned, or when he is learning to associate pairs of nonsense syllables" (p. 1003). To document this argument, Kessel noted, for example, how Spence, in the same way as other behaviorists, treated higher mental processes as "confounding variables" and thus could maintain his behavioristic presuppositions by controlling the "confounding variables."

As was stated above, research results which are in harmony with a prevailing paradigm are generally viewed as acceptable whereas those which are inharmonious are generally viewed as not acceptable. This was illustrated in a recent study by Goodstein and Brazis (1970). These investigators mailed to a random sample of psychologists virtually identical abstracts of presumably empirical research on astrology. The abstracts differed in only one respect: half reported positive findings and half negative findings. Even though the purported design of the study was identical for the two sets of abstracts, psychologists receiving the abstract reporting negative findings about astrology rated the study as better designed, more valid, and as having more adequate conclusions than those receiving the abstract reporting positive findings.

There is evidence indicating that the investigator's viewpoint and his degree of orthodoxy, that is, his acceptance of a dominant paradigm, influences the editor's or the referee's decision to accept or reject his article for publication in a scientific journal (Crane, 1967; Mahoney, 1975). However, very few studies have been conducted pertaining to this kind of paradigm bias in editorial decisions and this is an important area for further research.[1]

Although much has been said during recent years about how experimenters bias their results, comparatively little has been said about how investigators bias their results. Investigators bias their results, in accordance with their paradigm and correlated theories, at practically all stages of the research process. At the very beginning of the research there is bias in the questions that are asked and the hypotheses that are formulated. Each aspect of the research—e.g., the experimental design, the choice of subjects, the selection and training of experimenters, the analysis of data—is also biased by the underlying paradigm. Finally, the interpretations and conclusions that are drawn from the data are closely related to the underlying paradigms and associated theories (Dunnette, 1966).[2]

PARADIGMS VERSUS PET THEORIES OR HYPOTHESES

As stated above, *paradigms* refer to *general* beliefs and methods that are shared by many scientists at a given time, for example, the behavioristic and the Freudian paradigms in psychology. Also, as stated above, investigators who adhere to a particular paradigm tend to bias their studies in line with the paradigm in many ways—in the kinds of questions that they ask, in the methods they use to answer the questions, and in the way they interpret their data. A rather different kind of bias is also present within any one paradigm. Within a paradigm, investigators inevitably differ from each other by favoring different theories or hypotheses. Although the biasing effects of the general paradigm are difficult to see and difficult to take into account, the biasing effects of pet theories or hypotheses within any one paradigm are more easily seen. Relevant data were provided by Mitroff (1974) who interviewed 42 lunar scientists, asking questions such as, "Do scientists have to be committed to their ideas?" and, "Is commitment a threat to objectivity?" He reported the following:

> Of the 42 scientists interviewed, every one indicated that he thought the notion of the purely objective, uncommited scientist was naive . . . To the credit of these scientists, they not only freely acknowledged their biases but also argued that in order to be a good scientist, one *had* to have biases. The best scientist, they said, not only has points of view but also defends them with gusto. Their concept of a scientist did not imply that he would cheat by making up experimental data or falsifying it; rather he does everything in his power to defend his pet hypotheses against early and perhaps unwarranted death caused by the introduction of fluke data. The objectivity of science is a result, the scientists said, not of each individual scientist's unbiased outlook, but of the scientific community's examination and debate over the merits of respective biases. (p. 65)

An important proviso here, however, is that although the scientific community is ready to debate the merits of respective biases *within an accepted paradigm*, the biases that are inherent in the paradigm itself are much more difficult to see and to debate. For instance, the materialistic paradigm that underlies all science has practically never been criticized by scientists even though the basic tenets of materialism have been seriously questioned by philosophers at least since the days of Plato (Taylor, 1972).

RECOMMENDATIONS AND CONCLUSIONS

Of course, investigators cannot carry out research without having some basic assumptions and a way of conceptualizing the area of inquiry. Although a paradigm and associated theories are necessary for the conduct of research, investigators can become more aware of their underlying paradigm and can try to make their assumptions more explicit (Barber, 1970b; Chaves, 1968; Spanos, 1970; Spanos & Chaves, 1970).

The training of scientists should include more focused concern on the history of the sciences. The emphasis should be placed on how the accepted notions of physical, biological, and behavioral sciences have varied over time and how "facts" and "knowledge" were always relative to the preconceptions, assumptions, and paradigms that existed at a given time (Brush, 1974).

As Ziman (1968) pointed out, "the major task, and the corresponding problem of scientific education is easily defined; it must teach the consensus without turning it into an orthodoxy. The student must become perfectly familiar and at ease with the current state of knowledge and yet ready to overthrow it, from within" (p. 69). The problem, as stated by Sjoberg and Nett (1968), that must be squarely faced by the teachers of psychologists and other scientists, is "to balance off the need for sound, tested knowledge against the need for new and 'deviant' ideas in science" (p. 339).

Certainly, graduate training of psychologists and other scientists should include greater emphasis on the bias that is associated with paradigms and theories. As Dunnette (1966), McGuire (1973), and Sherif (1970) have pointed out, too many psychologists try to prove rather than modify their theories and when investigators are committed to a theory there tends to be a "unconscious" focusing on data which support the theory and a relative neglect of data that are not in harmony with the theory.

Dunnette (1966) has also recommended that some of the problems associated with the Investigator Paradigm Effect can be mollified if psychologists are taught thoroughly to test multiple alternative hypotheses rather than their one preferred hypothesis. Dunnette described this approach, which was originally formulated by Platt (1964), as follows:

> The approach entails devising multiple hypotheses to explain observed phenomena, devising crucial experiments each of which may exclude or disprove one or more of the hypotheses, and continuing with the retained hypotheses to refine the possibilities that remain ... One might say that the research emphasis is one of 'studying hypotheses' as opposed to 'substantiating theories'. (p. 350)

NOTES

1. Another general problem in the publication of research findings is due to an institutionalized norm: "scientists are expected to focus their reports on the logical structure of the methods used and ... are praised for presenting their research in a way that is elegantly bare of anything that does not serve this primary function and are deterred from reporting 'irrelevant' social and psychological aspects of the research process" (B. Barber & Fox, 1958, p. 525).

Scientific papers thus do not report potentially important components of the experimental research and thus tend to distort what actually goes on during the research process.

2. When experiments are reviewed in articles or textbooks, a process of "leveling, sharpening, and assimilation" commonly occurs which produces a simplified interpretation tending to be in harmony with the reviewer's assumptions and preconceptions. Interesting examples of how complex research findings are simplified in a biased way in textbooks and review articles are presented by Berkowitz (1971) and Yarrow, Campbell, and Burton (1968, pp. 132-133).

Pitfall II
Investigator Experimental Design Effect

Investigators who adhere to the same paradigm and who hold similar theories may nevertheless obtain dissimilar results and draw divergent conclusions because they design their experiments differently or carry out different kinds of studies. Denzin (1970) noted that the way the study is conducted will, in part, determine the results:

> Suppose that the same empirical situation is selected—for example, a mental hospital. The first investigator adopts the survey as his method; the second, participant observation. Each will make different kinds of observations, engage in different analyses, ask different questions, and—as a result—may reach different conclusions. (Of course the fact that they adopted different methods is not the only reason they will reach different conclusions. Their personalities, their values, and their choices of different theories will also contribute to this result.) (p. 12)

To illustrate the contention that the results of an experimental study can depend on the experimental design, I shall briefly discuss in turn (a) the complexity of the design, (b) whether the design takes account of sex differences, and (c) whether the experiment utilizes a same-subjects design or a randomized groups design.

Simple experimental designs are likely to yield simple results whereas more complex designs, such as factorial designs, are more likely to yield complex results that can negate the conclusions from

13

studies using simple designs. To illustrate this contention let us look briefly at hypnosis research. During the late 1920's and early 1930's, Clark Hull was the leading investigator in this area. He typically used a very simple experimental design in which the subjects' performance was assessed under an awake condition and after they had been exposed to a hypnotic induction procedure. Hull (1933) concluded from his experiments that responsiveness to suggestions was markedly higher under hypnotic trance as compared to the waking condition. Later experiments were conducted by others which included a third experimental condition; the subjects were tested either under a hypnotic condition, an awake condition, or an additional condition in which they were urged to try to perform to the best of their ability and to try to imagine vividly those things that were suggested (task motivational condition). In general, the results of these studies indicated that under the task-motivational condition the subjects were as responsive to suggestions as under the hypnotic induction condition (Barber, 1969a). Further experiments were then conducted which used factorial designs that simultaneously assessed the independent effects and the interactions of several variables. These experiments with more complex designs obtained more complex results. How subjects performed in hypnotic experiments was found to be affected by numerous variables such as how the situation was defined to the subjects, the wording and tone of the suggestions or instructions, subjects' attitudes toward "hypnosis", and subjects' expectancies concerning their own performances (Barber, 1969a, 1971a; Barber, Spanos, & Chaves, 1974). As the experiments became more complex by including more variables in factorial designs, the data and conclusions changed and "hypnotic trance" could no longer be viewed as simply as in the days when simple experimental designs were employed.

Experimental designs which consider the results for male and female subjects separately commonly yield results which differ from those which lump the results for males and females together. The effects of sex differences on experimental results were demonstrated by Carlson (1971) when she reviewed the papers published during 1968 in the *Journal of Personality* and the *Journal of Personality and Social Psychology*. Carlson noted that "Among the studies that could have tested for sex differences less than half reported such tests. Yet in 51 studies where sex differences *were* examined, significant effects of sex were found in 74 percent of the studies" (p. 205).

Whether or not the investigator uses a same-subjects design or a randomized groups design can also affect his results and conclusions.

An experimental design in which one group of subjects is exposed to all of the experimental conditions (same subjects design) is clearly preferable for some problems, such as the effects of increasing amounts of practice on learning. However, in most experimental studies either the same subjects design can be used or different subjects can be randomly assigned to each treatment (randomized groups design). It is commonly assumed that the results obtained with the same subjects design are the same as would be obtained with the randomized groups design. This is not always so. For instance, Grice and Hunter (1964) showed, in experiments dealing with eyelid conditioning and with simple reaction time, that quite different results were obtained with the same subjects design and the randomized groups design.

Pereboom (1971) has given additional examples of how the experimental design, and also the scales used for measurement, can affect the results. For example, given certain kinds of variability in the data, the choice of a scale for a given response measure may reverse one's conclusions (Edgington, 1960). Similarly, the type of interactions obtained may depend upon the type of measurement scales that are used (Hays, 1963).

In brief, the way an investigator designs his experiment can affect the results he obtains. Investigators who design studies and those who utilize or review the studies of others should place greater emphasis on the fact that experimental results are dependent on the way the experiment was designed.

Pitfall III
Investigator Loose Procedure Effect

A third effect associated with the investigator—the Investigator Loose Procedure Effect—pertains to the degree of imprecision of the experimental script or protocol which gives the step-by-step details of the procedures to be used in the experiment. In rather rare instances, experiments do not have a formal protocol or standardized procedures. In these cases the investigator has a general idea how the experiment is to proceed, but the steps of the procedure are not planned or written out beforehand and the way the subjects are to be treated is not standardized.

An example of experiments that do not have a formal protocol can be taken from the area of hypnosis research (Barber, 1969a, 1970b). Prior to the advent of rigorous research in this area, the experimenters were instructed (by the investigators) that they were to hypnotize one group of subjects but not another group. Nothing was stated as to what was to be said to the subjects, how the hypnotizing was to be done, or how long the hypnotic procedures were to last. Of course, it is difficult to draw conclusions from experiments based on such loose protocols because the procedures can vary with the moment-to-moment predilections of the experimenter. A study based on such imprecise procedures is unscientific in that science is based on the premise that the procedures of an experiment are specified in sufficient detail so that they can be replicated in other laboratories. If the procedures are imprecise, other laboratories cannot proceed to replicate them and to cross-validate the results.

In a somewhat more common case than the one described above, the experimental protocol has more precise specifications as to how the experiment is to be conducted, but there is still much missing and there is room for the experimenter to vary the procedure from subject to subject. For instance, experiments in psychology are, at times, based on experimental protocols which state that certain kinds of questions are to be answered by the subjects but the protocols do not state what is to be done if the subjects do not understand or misunderstand the questions. This failure to plan for contingencies is also found in loose protocols that do not state what the experimenter is to do at various steps in the procedure—for instance, how he is to interact with the subject immediately before he begins the experiment, what the experimenter is to do if the subject interrupts the experimental procedure because he wishes to smoke a cigarette, or how the experimenter is to carry out a specific test or interview procedure. The data from experiments that are based on loose experimental procedures are often reported very precisely. However, since the precise data are based on loose procedures that leave much room for bias, they can be misleading.

Loose experimental procedures can give rise to unreliable results. For instance, Feldman, Hyman, and Hart (1951) showed that experimenters obtain dissimilar data when there is a loose procedure (when they are permitted latitude in the way they word the questions that are submitted to the subjects). However, the same investigators also showed that experimenters obtain very similar data when the procedure is well structured (when the wording of the questions is clearly specified beforehand).

Raffetto (1967) has recently reported a study which illustrates the Investigator Loose Procedure Effect. The study was concerned with the effects of the experimenters' expectancies on reports of sensory experiences and hallucinations elicited in a sensory deprivation situation. Some of the experimenters were led to expect (by the investigator) that sensory deprivation produces many reports of sensory experiences and hallucinations, while other experimenters were led to expect that sensory deprivation produces few such reports. After each subject had undergone a period of sensory deprivation, he was interviewed by an experimenter. During these experimental interviews, experimenters expecting many reports of sensory experiences and hallucinations elicited more reports of this kind than experimenters expecting few such reports.

Raffetto's data indicated that the experimenters influenced their subjects reports because the experimental procedures were very loose—the interviews were not standardized and the experimenters conducted their interviews in different ways. As compared to experimenters expecting few reports of sensory experience and hallucinations, experimenters expecting many such reports more often encouraged their subjects to continue talking about their experiences, were much more active interviewers, and held much longer interviews. Thus it appears that when the investigator constructs a loose experiment and allows the experimenter to vary how he conducts the study, experimenters may conduct the study differently with subjects from whom they expect different responses, and this variability can affect the results.

In brief, if the investigator constructs a loose protocol and allows the experimenters to vary how they conduct the experimental procedures or interviews with different subjects, it is likely that the results of the experiment will be misleading. Investigators should make greater efforts to tighten their procedures and to avoid the Investigator Loose Procedure Effect.

Pitfall IV
Investigator Data Analysis Effect

The investigator's responsibility extends beyond deciding the kind of study to undertake, the kinds of data to gather, the type of experimental design to use, and the specific instructions and procedures to employ in the experiment. The investigator also has control of and is responsible for the data analysis even though the actual computations may be performed by an assistant or a computer. This phase of the research can easily give rise to an Investigator Data Analysis Effect.

Careful checks of statistical procedures by knowledgeable reviewers (e.g., Chapanis, 1963, pp. 310-313) at times reveal serious mistakes in the statistical analyses used in research reports which invalidate the conclusions. A survey by Wolins (1962) similarly indicated that inappropriate data analysis may not be uncommon and raised questions about investigators' willingness to permit reanalysis of their original data. Wolins asked 37 psychologists, who had recently published journal articles, for their original data. Twenty-six of the 37 (70 percent) did not reply or claimed that their original data were either lost, misplaced, or inadvertently destroyed. Finally, Wolins was able to reanalyze seven sets of data supplied by five investigators. Of the seven analyses, three involved gross errors. These errors were sufficiently great to change the conclusions reported in the journal articles. For instance, in one analysis several F ratios near one (which were clearly nonsignificant) were reported to be highly significant, and another F ratio was incorrectly reported to be nonsignificant due to the use of an inappropriate error term.

A decade later, Craig and Reese (1973) found an improvement in investigators' willingness to show their original data but they did not ascertain whether errors in statistical analysis had decreased. They wrote to 53 authors of articles published during one month in four psychological journals and asked for copies of their original data to be used in a master's thesis.[1] Of the 53 authors who received letters, 8 did not reply, 9 completely refused to share their data, 5 reported that the data were currently unavailable, and 4 indicated that the data had been lost or destroyed. However, the results were more encouraging than those reported a decade earlier by Wolins (1962); Craig and Reese (1973) reported that about half of the authors (27 of 53) who received letters requesting their data cooperated to some degree—20 sent their data or a summary analysis and 7 offered data if they were provided with further information.

Let us now look at eight types of data analyses that can produce biased results. Although these eight pitfalls in analyzing data tend to be overlapping, they can be best clarified by discussing them separately.

1. A serious potential pitfall is present when investigators collect a large amount of data and have not pre-planned how they are to analyze the data. Lipset, Trow, and Coleman (1970) have emphasized this pitfall, noting that "If [an investigator] is blessed with an abundance of data . . . he can select those data which confirm his hypothesis that a relationship exists" [p. 83]. The major problem here is that the investigator decides how the data are to be analyzed after he has "eyeballed" or studied the data. After the investigator has perused the data, he may decide to analyze only certain parts of the data while neglecting other parts. When the investigator has not planned the data analysis *beforehand*, he may find it difficult to avoid the pitfall of focusing only on the data which look promising (or which meet his expectations or desires) while neglecting data which do not seem "right" (which are incongruous with his assumptions, desires, or expectations). When not planned beforehand, data analysis can approximate a projective technique, such as the Rorschach, because the investigator can project on the data his own expectancies, desires, or biases and can pull out of the data almost any "findings" he may desire.

2. Investigators at times fail to report that the data did not support their original hypothesis. Instead, after they have studied the data, they derive a new hypothesis that is supported by the data and then "verify" the new hypothesis by performing a statistical test on

the same data from which it was derived (Lipset, Trow, & Coleman, 1970; Selvin, 1970). Although investigators may derive a new hypothesis from a completed study, the new hypothesis needs to be tested and verified in a subsequent study.

3. Investigators at times collect incidental data that are not directly related to the hypotheses they are testing. If they fail to confirm their original hypotheses, they then perform a large number of statistical tests on the remaining data and report whatever significant results are obtained as "findings." The rationale behind this procedure seems to be "If we don't get significant results on the variables we are interested in, then we'll have these other variables to fall back on and we'll have something 'positive' to report." These kinds of procedures can easily lead to misleading conclusions. In the next section of this chapter we shall look carefully at a report that illustrates this kind of pitfall in data analysis.

4. At times investigators conduct post-mortem analyses on the same data after the originally-intended analyses have been performed and have failed to yield significant findings. This misleading procedure typically involves cutting or slicing the data in originally unintended ways. This kind of post-mortem analysis can provide hypotheses to be tested in further research but it leads to misleading conclusions when the results are accepted without replication. The reason why post-mortem data analyses lead to misleading conclusions is that random numbers will yield statistically significant "findings" if they are cut or subdivided in various ways and subjected to statistical analysis. This kind of Investigator Data Analysis Effect is not uncommon in psychological research (Clement, 1972) and we shall present an example of this pitfall in the next section of this chapter.

5. Investigators at times perform a large number of statistical tests and find that a small number, say 5 percent, are significant at the .05 level. The "significant" results are then reported without consideration of the fact that at least 5 percent of the comparisons will be significant at the .05 level by chance alone.

6. Investigators at times "report from among a sizable number of computed comparisons only those that are significant [but the] reader is not told about this selection" (McNemar, 1960). Of course, when many statistical tests are performed on a set of data, the alpha rate changes considerably (Blanchard, 1971). Feild and Armenakis (1974) have clearly demonstrated how multiple tests of significance can easily lead to erroneous conclusions. For instance, they state: "Suppose an investigator set his significance level at .05 and con-

ducted 10 independent tests. He may think that his probability of Type I error [rejecting a null hypothesis when it is true] is .05. However, his actual probability of Type I error in one or more of the 10 decisions is .40" (p. 428). Neher (1967) has labeled this pitfall as *probability pyramiding* and has commented as follows:

> Reporting the 5 percent level for a finding means that there is only a 5 percent chance that it is a spurious finding resulting solely from chance variations. If, however, two independent analyses are done, the probability that at least one such analysis will yield a spurious 'significant finding' at this level is greater than 5 percent. (The assumption of independence of the two analyses, while not always true, simplifies the discussion without introducing serious error.) To determine the new probability level, one may calculate the probability that a significant result would not be obtained in either of the two tries (.95 X .95) and then subtract this from 1. Thus, $1-(.95)^2 = 1-.902 = .098$. If three independent analyses are done, the real level becomes $1-(.95)^3 = 1-.857 = .143$. (Each individual analysis increases the probability pyramiding, even though it may be part of one large 'analysis', such as stepwise multiple regression, item analysis, etc.). (p. 259)

7. Related problems arise when an investigator obtains negative results (or fails to confirm his hypothesis) and then fails to report his negative results. In an interesting paper, Dunnette (1966) described his personal experiences which led him to "become aware of the massive size of this graveyard for dead studies . . ." (p. 347). Similarly, McNemar (1960) noted that investigators at times "simply discard all data of an experiment as bad data if not in agreement with theory, and start over." The problem here is that if the investigator obtains positive results in a later study and publishes them without mentioning his earlier negative results, the reader is likely to conclude wrongly that the positive results are more stable, more easily replicable, or more valid than is actually the case. Rhine (1974b) has appropriately pointed out that, "The subtle private judgments about what data to 'declare' in reporting constitute an area that needs the fullest possible safeguarding" (p. 110).

8. When an investigator obtains negative results that fail to confirm his hypothesis he is likely to check for computational errors in the data analysis or to run another data analysis (Friedlander, 1964). However, when the original analysis confirms the investigators' hypothesis, it is unlikely that he will check for computational errors or run another analysis. To illustrate these pitfalls, Friedlander

(1964) courageously offered himself as an example, describing how he looked for mistakes in the data analysis when it yielded results that contradicted his expectations. He concluded that research investigators tend to accept the adage, "If you don't succeed at first, try and try again", and they also accept the adage, "If you *do* succeed at first, do not try again" (p. 199).

9. At times, investigators place heavy emphasis upon a statistically significant outcome but fail to point out that the degree or strength of association between the two variables is actually very small or negligible (Kish, 1970). A significant value of F, t, or chi-square means that probably there is some dependence between the variables in the population, but the degree of dependence may be practically zero *regardless of the significance level* (Duggan & Dean, 1968). Kish (1970) appropriately pointed out that, "The results of statistical 'tests of significance' are functions not only of the magnitude of the relationships studied but also of the number of sampling units used (and the efficiency of design). In small samples, significant, that is, meaninfgul results may fail to appear 'statistically significant.' But if the sample is large enough the most insignificant relationships will appear 'statistically significant' " (pp. 138-139). There are several ways to avoid this pitfall. Instead of presenting results in terms of tests of significance, they could be presented in terms of confidence intervals (Natrella, 1960). Probably a better way of avoiding the pitfall is to present an estimate of the strength of association along with the statistical test of significance (Dunnette, 1966, p. 350). Such measures of degree or strength of association include, for example, Goodman and Kurskal's *gamma* for chi-square, r^2 for Pearsonian correlations, omega squared, and many others that are discussed by Cohen (1965), Fleiss (1969), and Keppel (1973, Chap. 25).[2]

PITFALLS IN DATA ANALYSIS:
TWO ILLUSTRATIVE STUDIES

To illustrate the pitfalls that were listed above, we shall analyze two important and influential studies that are directly pertinent to the topic of this book. The two illustrative studies aimed to demonstrate one of the major pitfalls discussed in this text (Pitfall X), namely, that experimenters unintentionally and subtly communicate their expectancies to their subjects and the subjects respond in accordance with the experimenters' expectancies (Experimenter Unintentional Expectancy Effect). Paradoxically, while trying to demonstrate one of the major pitfalls, the Experimenter Unintentional Expectancy Effect, these studies seem to demonstrate another one of the major pitfalls, the Investigator Data Analysis Effect.

Illustrative Study 1

In the first study (Rosenthal, Persinger, Mulry, Vikan-Kline, & Grothe, 1964b), 20 student experimenters were asked to test a total of 73 subjects on Rosenthal's person-perception task. When using this task, the subject is shown a series of photographed faces. The subject is asked to rate on a numerical scale whether each of the individuals shown on the photographs has been experiencing success (high ratings) or has been experiencing failure (low ratings).

The study was designed to show that experimenters obtain ratings from their subjects that they expect to obtain. To induce the student experimenters to expect high (or low) ratings from their subjects on the person-perception task, each experimenter was told (by an investigator) that, on the basis of personality tests given to the subjects, it could be expected that certain of their subjects would perceive the photographed individuals as successful (high ratings) and other specified subjects would see them as failures (low ratings). (Since the subjects were *not* given the personality tests and were randomly assigned to the experimenters, the subjects should not actually differ in their ratings.) The dependent variable was the difference between the average ratings obtained by each experimenter from those subjects whom he expected would give high ratings and those subjects whom he expected would give low ratings.

The investigators (Rosenthal et al., 1964b) did not perform an overall statistical analysis of the data to determine if the subjects' ratings were harmonious with the experimenters' induced expectancies for high or low ratings. Instead of determining first whether the data showed the hypothesized Experimenter Unintentional Expectancy Effect, the investigators stated first that 3 of the 20 experimenters showed a "reversal of the biasing effect of expectancy, i.e., they obtained data significantly opposite to what they had been led to expect." The investigators then analyzed the data for the remaining 17 experimenters and reported that these experimenters showed a significant Experimenter Unintentional Expectancy Effect, that is, they obtained ratings from their subjects in line with their (the experimenters') expectancies.

There are several interrelated reasons why this conclusion—that the study showed an Experimenter Unintentional Expectancy Effect—cannot be accepted as valid: (a) The investigators concluded that the effect was present after performing an analysis that did not include the negative data (in the opposite direction) that were obtained by 3 of the 17 experimenters. (b) The negative data were excluded from the analysis (which supposedly showed the Experimenter Unintentional Expectancy Effect) after the investigators had inspected the data and after they had determined that some of the data were negative with respect to the experimental hypothesis. (c) The investigators were *not* using the acceptable procedure of excluding data by means of a criterion that was determined *prior* to inspection of the data. (d) The way the data were analyzed did not allow for the possibility that the study may have simply failed to show an Experimenter Unintentional Expectancy Effect. In another connection, Chapanis and Chapanis (1964) presented several reasons why these kinds of statistical procedures lead to misleading conclusions:

> Unfortunately, this line of reasoning [that data which are counter to the hypothesis can be excluded from the analysis which aims to test the hypothesis] contains one fundamental flaw: *it does not allow the possibility that the null hypothesis may be correct.* The [investigator], in effect, is asserting that his . . . prediction is correct and that *S*s who do not conform to the prediction should be excluded from the analysis. This is a foolproof method of guaranteeing positive results.
>
> Some people may feel that no matter how questionable the selection procedure, it must still mean something if it leads to significant results. This point of view, however, cannot be reconciled with the following facts of life: it is always possible to obtain a significant difference between two columns of figures in a table of random numbers provided we use the appropriate scheme for rejecting certain of these numbers . . .
>
> We strongly recommend that *S*s not be discarded from the sample *after* data collection and inspection of the results. Nor is it methodologically sound to reject *S*s whose results do not conform to the prediction . . . If there are any theoretical grounds for suspecting that some *S*s will not show the predicted . . . effect, the characteristics of such *S*s, or the conditions, should be specifiable in advance. It should then be possible to do an analysis on all *S*s by dividing them into two groups, those predicted to show [the effect] and those predicted not to show it . (pp. 16-17)

In brief, no confidence can be placed in research reports that conclude that the hypothesis was confirmed by a statistical analysis which excluded the data that were judged, after inspection of the results, to be significantly opposite to the hypothesis. When the data of the study are analyzed appropriately using all 20 experimenters, there is no significant difference between the ratings obtained when the experimenters expected high ratings and when they expected low ratings.

Illustrative Study 2

We shall further illustrate the Investigator Data Analysis Effect by looking closely at a widely quoted study (Rosenthal, Persinger, Vikan-Kline, & Mulry, 1963) which aimed to demonstrate that (a) experimenters unintentionally communicate their expectancies to their subjects, (b) the subjects then respond in accordance with the experimenters' expectancies, (c) experimenters also unintentionally communicate their expectancies to their assistants, and (d) when the assistants henceforth test subjects, they also unintentionally obtain data in line with their expectancies.

There were 14 experimenters in the study who tested 76 subjects on the person-perception task. Each experimenter later trained two assistants and the 28 assistants then tested 154 additional subjects on the same task. The three major independent variables were as follows:

1. The experimenters first stated the average ratings they expected to obtain from their subjects on the person-perception task. These expectancies were termed the experimenters' *idiosyncratic expectancies* or biases.

2. Before testing their subjects, half of the experimenters were told (by the investigator) that they should expect to obtain high ("success") ratings from their subjects and half were told that they should expect to obtain low ("failure") ratings and they were given a rationale why they should expect to obtain such ratings. These expectations were labeled as *induced expectancies.*

3. Subsequently, the experimenters were led to expect (by the investigator) that their assistants would obtain the same high (or low) ratings from their subjects that they (the experimenters) had been originally led to expect. However, the investigator warned the experimenters not to tell their assistants what type of ratings they should expect. After the assistants had tested their subjects, analyses were performed to determine if the assistants obtained ratings which were in line with either the idiosyncratic or induced expectancies of

the experimenters who had originally trained them.

The major dependent variables in this study were the ratings on the person-perception task given by the subjects tested by the experimenters and by the subjects tested by the assistants. The authors of the paper reported that "The 2 X 2 analysis of variance, based on Es' Ss' ratings as a function of Es' induced and idiosyncratic [expectancy] bias yielded no F with an associated $p < .15$" [p. 321]. This statement means that the Experimenter Unintentional Expectancy Effect was not demonstrated in this study—the experimenters did not obtain ratings from their subjects which agreed with what the experimenters originally expected to obtain (idiosyncratic expectancies) or what the investigator told them to expect (induced expectancies). In addition, the authors of this paper presented an analysis of variance which indicated that the assistants were *not* significantly influenced by their experimenters to obtain ratings in accord with the experimenters' idiosyncratic or induced expectancies.

The conclusion indicated by the analyses mentioned above is that the study had not demonstrated an Experimenter Unintentional Expectancy Effect and also had not demonstrated an Assistant Unintentional Expectancy Effect—that is, neither the experimenters' nor the assistants' expectancies had influenced their subjects' ratings on the person-perception task. The investigators (Rosenthal et al., 1963), however, failed to draw the conclusion that the study had failed to demonstrate expectancy effects. Instead, they went on to perform additional statistical analyses among the variables mentioned above and many other variables. We shall now summarize Barber and Silver's (1968a, 1968b) critique of these additional analyses in order to illustrate several types of Investigator Data Analyses Effects.

1. These additional statistical analyses took into consideration at least 22 independent variables and 4 dependent variables. The 22 independent variables included, for example, the experimenters' and the assistants' idiosyncratic and induced expectancies and a variety of personality characteristics of the experimenters, the assistants, and the subjects. The 4 dependent variables included two methods for measuring the effects of the experimenters' expectancies and two methods for measuring the effects of the assistants' expectancies.

2. When a study includes many independent and many dependent variables, the investigator should perform a multivariate analysis (e.g., factor analysis, multiple-discriminant analysis, canonical correlation, multivariate analysis of variance or covariance). A multivariate analysis applied to multivariate data can yield unambiguous conclusions concerning the effects of the independent variables on

the dependent variables. However, if a multivariate analysis is not performed—if the investigator analyzes the data bit-by-bit (for example, analyzes the effects of one or more independent variables separately on each dependent variable)—serious problems of probability pyramiding arise (Neher, 1967).

3. The investigators (Rosenthal et al., 1963) did not perform a multivariate analysis and, in fact, could not do so because such an analysis requires a very large number of subjects.

4. Although the 22 independent variables and the 4 dependent variables could give rise to thousands of possible statistical comparisons (Guilford, 1954, p. 80), the investigators analyzed only a small fraction of the data bit-by-bit, utilizing primarily t tests and Spearman $rhos$. The investigators performed about 125 statistical comparisons of which about 21 were significant at the .05 level.

5. If the investigators had made *planned comparisons* (that is, if they had specified in advance which comparisons were to be made), and if each comparison was independent of the others, one would expect at least 6 of the 125 to be "significant" at the .05 level by chance alone.

6. However, since the investigators were not making planned comparisons and since at least 5 percent of the thousands of possible comparisons that were present in the data could be expected to be "significant" at the .05 level by chance alone, it is difficult to determine exactly how many of the 125 comparisons (that were selected by unclear criteria from the thousands of possible comparisons) might be "significant" by chance alone but this number could easily have exceeded 21 (cf., Hays, 1963, Chap. 14).

7. Furthermore, of the 21 comparisons that were found to be nominally "significant," about 15 involved overlapping data. When separate statistical tests are made on overlapping sets of data, it can be expected that if one set is significant the other set (which includes much of the same data) may also be significant and the two statistics cannot be considered as independent of each other. When the statistical comparisons are not independent, the percentage of comparisons that can be expected to be significant at the .05 level by chance alone far exceeds 5 percent.

8. Of the remaining 6 nominally significant statistics, 5 were t tests that were performed upon data which had been first tested for significance by overall F tests. The F tests failed to show significant effects and the null hypothesis should have been accepted. When the preliminary analysis of variance does not show overall significance, post-mortem analyses of the same data by means of t tests yields

uninterpretable results (Hays, 1963, p. 483).

In brief, although this study (Rosenthal et al., 1963) was interpreted as showing an Experimenter Unintentional Expectancy Effect and also an Assistant Unintentional Expectancy Effect, the interpretation was not valid. The study was inappropriately analyzed and the investigators drew conclusions that were not justified by the data—that is, the conclusions were based on an Investigator Data Analysis Effect.[3]

SUMMARY

Let us now summarize some of the Investigator Data Analysis Effects that were found in the two illustrative studies described above.

In the first study, (a) an overall statistical analysis was not performed to reject the null hypothesis, (b) negative data (data which were significantly opposite to the experimental hypothesis) were not used in the statistical analysis which supposedly confirmed the experimental hypothesis, and (c) the decision not to use the negative data was made after inspection of the results and without a predetermined rationale.

Some of the pitfalls in the second study were as follows: (a) After an overall analysis had failed to reject the null hypothesis at a conventional level of significance, the investigators performed a large number of post-mortem statistical tests on the data. The investigators failed to make clear that the results of such post-mortem analyses are far from definitive and can, at best, only suggest new hypotheses to be validated in further research. (b) Problems of probability pyramiding were not avoided (Neher, 1967); for example, there was a failure to take account of changing levels of significance when many statistical tests were performed on a single set of data (Feild & Armenakis, 1974; Ryan, 1959). (c) The investigators strained for significance by accepting p values greater than .10 as confirming the experimental hypothesis. (d) The investigators failed to perform a multivariate statistical analysis, such as multiple analysis of variance, in a study which included many independent and many dependent variables. Instead, a large number of comparisons were made on overlapping data by individual t tests and Spearman rhos.

RECOMMENDATIONS

The above considerations suggest that some of the many ways that an investigator can avoid an Investigator Data Analysis Effect is to adhere to the following principles:

1. If the investigator is not using the technique of planned comparisons—that is, if the particular comparisons that are to be made are not specified in advance (Hays, 1963, Chap. 14)— an overall statistical test should be performed that includes *all* of the data.

2. The probability value required for rejection of the null hypothesis should be specified in advance.

3. Conclusions should not be drawn from the results of post-mortem tests performed upon the data after an overall test has failed to reject the null hypothesis. The results of such post-mortem tests should be "substantiated in independent research in which they are specifically predicted and tested" (Kerlinger, 1964, p. 621).

4. The statistical analyses should avoid errors of probability pyramiding (Feild & Armenakis, 1974; Neher, 1967), for example, the error of "finding some significant F ratios in an experiment by complicating the experiment with more and more irrelevant variables, while continuing to base the error rate upon the individual F" (Ryan, 1959).

5. If many independent and many dependent variables are used in one study, they should be clearly specified before hand, a large number of subjects should be used (so that there are sufficient numbers of subjects in each cell of the experimental design), and the data should be analyzed by multivariate procedures such as multiple-discriminant analysis, multivariate analysis of variance or covariance, canonical correlation, or factor analysis. The analysis of multivariate studies should not be carried out piecemeal by individual t tests, Spearman *rhos*, chi-squares, etc. (Cattell, 1966).

6. Instead of including many independent and dependent variables in a study (which requires a large number of subjects if the investigator is to carry out an appropriate multivariate analysis), the investigator might consider the advantages of keeping the number of variables within manageable proportions. As Hays (1963) cogently pointed out:

> In planning an experiment, it is a temptation to throw in many experimental treatments, especially if the data are inexpensive and the experimenter is adventuresome. However, this is *not* always good policy

if the psychologist is interested in finding meaning in his results, other things being equal, the simpler the psychological experiment the better will be its execution, and the more likely will one be able to decide what actually happened and what the results actually mean. (p. 411)

MOTIVATIONS FOR POSITIVE RESULTS

To reduce the extent of the Investigator Data Analysis Effect, it is necessary to emphasize in the training of behavioral scientists how and why this effect exists and how investigators should take pains to avoid it. Of course, this depends primarily on our teachers in psychology and the behavioral sciences and their willingness to talk about this effect openly and to continuously caution their students about it.

Although the Investigator Data Analysis Effect can be reduced by bringing it out from behind closed doors and talking about it openly, nevertheless, there are strong motivations that tend to give rise to this effect and, as long as they exist, we can expect the effect to occur. To further reduce the prevalence of this effect it is necessary to remove the motivations. One of these motivations derives from the belief that investigators will not be able to publish their research in professional journals if they do not report positive results. Let us look more closely at the complexities involved in publishing papers.

McNemar (1960) conjectured that studies with non-significant results are usually not submitted for publication; investigators commonly select their significant findings for inclusion in their reports. This conjecture was confirmed by Sterling (1959) when he surveyed all of the papers published during 1955 in four major psychological journals.[4] In 97 percent of the studies that used statistical tests, the null hypothesis was rejected, that is, "positive" findings were reported. More recently, Bozarth and Roberts (1972) checked all of the articles published from January 1967 to August 1970 in three journals concerned with counseling psychology[5] and Greenwald (1975) checked the articles published during 1972 in the *Journal of Personality and Social Psychology*. Bozarth and Roberts reported that, of the studies using statistical tests, 94 percent rejected the null hypothesis and Greenwald found that 88 percent of the articles reported positive results. It thus appears that nonsignificant results are either rarely submitted for publication and/or rarely accepted for publication.[6]

The implication of the above, that there exists a misleading selection of "significant" results for publication in journals, is supported by Cohen's (1962) analysis of papers published during 1960 in the *Journal of Abnormal and Social Psychology*. He analyzed 70 studies with regard to the power of the statistical tests that were used. (The power of a test is directly proportional to the size of the sample.) He found that the power of the tests, that is, the probability of rejecting the null hypothesis of no difference when there actually was a difference, was typically meager. That is, the size of the samples were typically too small to expect that the statistics would yield significant results very often even when the null hypothesis was false. However, with few exceptions, each of the 70 studies reported "significant" results even though the statistical tests were usually not sufficiently powerful to detect "significance" with the relatively small samples that were used. The results of Cohen's analysis can be interpreted as indicating either that (a) investigators "find" significance in their data even though their statistical tests are not sufficiently powerful to detect "significance" with the typically small samples that are used, (b) they select only their significant findings for publication and do not submit their negative findings, or (c) journal editors select the significant findings for publication and reject the negative findings.

In line with the above, Smart (1964) noted that there appear to be two main reasons why studies with negative results are rarely published: (a) Authors are more likely to submit their positive rather than their negative results for publication. (b) Negative results are subjected to more editorial scrutiny. Support for the latter contention is found in a recent investigation (Mahoney, 1975), and also in an editorial statement made by a former editor of the prestigious *Journal of Experimental Psychology*. The editor (A.W. Melton) stated that he was very reluctant to publish results that were not significant at the .01 level (Bakan, 1967). Smart (1964) noted the following problems that arise from these practices: (a) If researchers are aware of studies supporting a hypothesis but not those which did not support it, they are misled into believing that the hypothesis is more valid than is actually the case. (b) Without an awareness of negative results in an area, other investigators are unable to make improvements in their experimental designs which might lead to positive results. Another problem, which is not mentioned by Smart, is that the emphasis on positive results may lead investigators to perform inappropriate data analyses so as to obtain "positive" results.

The notion that journal editors tend to reject reports of negative results is true in some cases (see Melton's statement above), but this notion is also misleading. It is not negative results per se that are difficult to publish but results that are judged to be meaningless, trivial, or as failing to enhance understanding. Both negative results and positive results can fail to contribute to knowledge or theory or be meaningless or trivial. As stated in the *Publication Manual of the American Psychological Association* (Anonymous, 1974, p. 22), positive results with regard to a trivial question "or devoid of theoretical explanation" are practically as valueless as negative results with regard to the same question. Good research answers meaningful questions and a meaningful question can be answered either by Yes (positive results) or No (negative results). For example, in the area of hypnotism my co-workers and I have asked, Is a standardized hypnotic induction procedure more effective than brief task-motivational instructions in enhancing responsiveness to test suggestions as measured by the Barber Suggestibility Scale? Although a series of experiments provided a "No" answer to this question (negative results), they were all readily publishable because they answered an important question (Barber, 1969a). As the *Publication Manual of the APA* (Anonymous, 1974) states, negative results are of interest to editors (a) "when an established theory clearly predicts that a difference or correlation should be found" and also (b) "when an investigator discovers a methodological weakness in a published report of positive results and, correcting the weakness, finds that the significances vanish" [p. 21].

In brief, the major problem is *not* in the results but in the questions that are to be answered. If investigators asked meaningful questions, the answers to the questions would themselves be meaningful regardless of whether the answer is Yes (positive results) or No (negative results). However, the notion that negative results are difficult to publish has a basis of truth. Not all negative results but certain types of negative results are difficult to publish. The type of negative results that are difficult to publish are specified as follows by the *Publication Manual of the APA* (Anonymous, 1974): "Failure to replicate results of a previous investigator, using the same method but a different sample, is generally of questionable value. A single failure may merely testify to sampling errors or to the conclusion that one of the two samples had unique characteristics responsible for the reported effect, or the lack of effect. An author can resolve the issue when he reports several failures with a range of samples. A single failure is too equivocal to justify publication on its merit alone" (pp. 21-22).

The above is related to a more general problem. When no relationship is found between an independent and a dependent variable, there are many reasons why we cannot conlcude that there is actually no relationship in addition to the statistical point that we can never prove the null hypothesis: for instance, the independent variable may not have been successfully manipulated and the measure of the dependent variable may have been inadequate (Mills, 1969).

Investigators could consider the problems associated with negative results within the following perspective: (a) Many questions, when answered, contribute to knowledge regardless of whether the answer is Yes (positive results) or No (negative results). (b) Many questions can be worded in a way that avoids the problem of negative results. For instance, instead of testing a null hypothesis, such as "Hypnosis is no more effective than task motivational instructions in enhancing response to suggestions," the question can be worded in such a way that either a Yes or a No answer is equally enlightening, for example, "Is a procedure that includes many components (a hypnotic induction procedure) more effective than one of its components (task motivational instructions) in raising suggestibility?"

After discussing problems similar to those delineated above, Greenwald (1975) came to similar conclusions: "1. Do research in which any outcome (including a null one) can be an acceptable and informative outcome. 2. Judge your own (or others') research not on the basis of the results but only on the basis of adequacy of procedures and importance of findings" (p. 19).[7]

NOTES

1. The journals were *Journal of Comparative and Physiological Psychology, Journal of Personality and Social Psychology, Journal of Verbal Learning and Verbal Behavior,* and *Journal of Educational Psychology.*

2. Lykken (1968) and also Minturn (1971) have presented an additional tongue-in-cheek solution to the related pitfall of confusing statistical significance with the potential replicability of results. They noted that the confidence that an investigator actually has in his findings may differ from the p values that he reports, because the investigator is aware of far more about his research than is reflected in his p values. Consequently, Lykken (1968) and Minturn (1971) proposed the "test of the gambler's challenge" or a "Wagers" section in journals where the author bets a certain amount of money on the repeatability of his results.

3. Most of the studies conducted prior to 1968 which were interpreted as demonstrating an Experimenter Unintentional Expectancy Effect (Rosenthal, 1966, 1968) did not actually show this effect; instead, many of the studies seemed to show an Investigator Data Analysis Effect (Barber, 1969b; Barber & Silver, 1968a, 1968b). A statistical analysis of 12 additional studies, which was interpreted as showing an Experimenter Modeling Effect (Rosenthal, 1966), was also inappropriate, that is, it also showed an Investigator Data Analysis Effect (Silver, 1968). Additional Investigator Data Analysis Effects have been delineated by Elashoff and Snow (1971) in their detailed critique of the kinds of data analyses that were used in the famous and influential book entitled *Pygmalion in the Classroom: Teacher Expectation and Pupils' Intellectual Development* (Rosenthal & Jacobson, 1968).

4. The journals were *Journal of Experimental Psychology, Journal of Comparative and Physiological Psychology, Journal of Clinical Psychology*, and *Journal of Social Psychology*.

5. The journals were *Personnel and Guidance Journal, Journal of Consulting and Clinical Psychology*, and *Journal of Counseling Psychology*.

6. In Sterling's (1959) survey, none of the 362 journal reports were replications of previous studies and, in the Bozarth and Roberts (1972) survey, less than 1 percent of the articles were replications of previous studies.

7. Greenwald (1975) also noted that there are several commonly accepted notions about the null hypothesis and about negative results that are misleading. One such notion is that since one cannot prove the null hypothesis, therefore, no conclusions can be drawn from negative results. Greenwald pointed out the misleading features of this contention as follows:

> The notion that you cannot prove the null hypothesis is true in the same sense that it is also true that you cannot prove *any* exact (or point) hypothesis. However, there is no reason for believing that an estimate of some parameter that is near a zero point is less valid than an estimate that is significantly different from zero. Currently available Bayesian techniques (e.g., Phillips, 1973) allow methods of describing acceptability of null hypothesis. (p. 2)

Greenwald (1975) next considered the argument that science advances by discovering relations between variables, that is, by rejecting the null hypothesis. He noted that "This argument ignores the fact that scientific advance if often most powerfully achieved by *rejecting* theories (cf., Platt, 1964). A major strategy for doing this is to demonstrate that relationships predicted by a theory are not obtained, and this would often require acceptance of a null hypothesis" (p. 2). After presenting a series of additional cogent arguments, Greenwald (1975) concluded that, "*Support for the null hypothesis must be regarded as a research outcome that is acceptable as any other*" (p. 16).

Pitfall V
Investigator Fudging Effect

For the sake of completeness, it is necessary to discuss a taboo topic—the Investigator Fudging Effect. This effect is present when an investigator intentionally reports results that are not the results he actually obtained. In this chapter, I shall first summarize some of the relevant data pertaining to the Investigator Fudging Effect and then I shall discuss the motivations and countermotivations for fudging.

SOME INSTANCES OF FUDGING

Newton, Dalton, Mendel

Although outright fraud (fudging of all or most of the data) is probably very rare in the behavioral sciences, "pushing the data", or letting desires and biases influence the way the data are analyzed or reported, may not be too rare. For instance, if an investigator finds that the statistical test of his hypothesis is approaching significance at, say, $p = .15$, he may fudge the p value by changing it to $p = .05$. This type of fudging has been noted by many students of Scientific history. For instance, after discussing instances of outright fraud in science, Merton (1957) noted that probably much more common are instances of "trimming" or "cooking" the data which are probably due to excessive concern with success in scientific work.

It appears that even Isaac Newton indulged in "small-scale"

fudging to make his data appear more precise than they actually were. Westfall (1973) presented a series of examples in which Newton's measurements matched his theoretical predictions to a degree of accuracy that was impossible at that time. Westfall commented as follows:

> And having proposed exact correlation as the criterion of truth, [Newton in his *Principia*] took care to see that exact correlation was presented, whether or not it was properly achieved. Not the least part of the *Principia's* persuasiveness was its deliberate pretense to a degree of precision quite beyond its legitimate claim. If the *Principia* established the quantitative pattern of modern science, it equally suggested a less sublime truth—that no one can manipulate the fudge factor quite so effectively as the master mathematician himself. (pp. 751-752)

Along similar lines, it appears that Dalton (or possibly his assistants) may have fudged some of his data on chemical atomism (Brush, 1974). Also, it appears that Mendel (or possibly his assistants) fudged some of his data on genetics (Brush, 1974). Relevant here is the demonstration by Ronald Fisher, the noted statistician, that the data in Mendel's original paper on heredity could *not* have been true "because it was inconceivable, short of an 'absolute miracle of chance', to obtain these ratios" (Koestler, 1971, p. 56). Questions pertaining to fudging of data have also arisen more recently in the sciences. Let us look at a representative case.

The Summerlin Case

William T. Summerlin, a scientist at the Sloan-Kettering Institute for Cancer Research, recently admitted fudging data in a very important investigation. This investigator had reported a series of studies indicating that, when skin and other organs are maintained for a time in tissue culture, they lose their ability to provoke an immune response. The important implication of these reports was that organs could be transplanted between genetically non-related individuals without the organ being rejected. Summerlin admitted that he had fudged data that he presented to the head of the institute. Specifically, he had painted the skin of two mice to make them falsely appear that they had been successfully grafted. Summerlin was also charged with irresponsible conduct by an investigating committee for misrepresenting other experiments which supposedly indicated successful transplants of human corneas (Culliton, 1974).

Faber (1974) cogently commented on the implications of the Summerlin case as follows:

> We are naive to believe that dishonesty in research is unique and aberrant. The rewards are just too tempting: prestige, ego enhancement, promotion, and, as in the case of Summerlin, a $40,000 salary and a home in Darien, Connecticut. Mighty tempting rewards for success. Not only are the rewards tempting but, while the process of socialization in graduate school may give credence to veracity, it nonetheless emphasizes success. The emphasis on scientific success creates a severe strain on the practicing researcher, who is torn between the norms established for the process of research and the penultimate rewards for success. Under these conditions deviance is likely to occur in any group, even among scientists. (p. 734)

Parapsychology

The problem of deception or fudging of the data has been especially critical for the area of parapsychology. Over the years, researchers in parapsychology have instituted a wide variety of controls which have met the criticisms that have been levelled at the field. However, when all other criticisms have been answered, there still remains one criticism that has prevented some scientists from fully accepting the findings from parapsychology. This criticism is simply that parapsychological researchers can produce significant ESP results by fudging a very small part of their data (Hansel, 1966; Price, 1955). Since scientists are aware that fudging a small part of the data to make the study "come out right" or to obtain statistically significant results is not too uncommon among their own associates, they can easily see this happening also in parapsychological research. Although scientists are aware that "small-scale" fudging occurs among their own colleagues, there are two reasons why they view this kind of fudging as more serious in parapsychology: (a) they believe ESP is inherently improbable or highly unlikely whereas they believe their own field is well-established. (b) They believe that, in their own field, replication of studies by independent laboratories determines the validity of original findings whereas, in the area of parapsychology, cross-validation by independent laboratories is very rare.

J.B. Rhine, who has been at the forefront of research in

parapsychology for many years, has once again demonstrated his role as a leader and ground-breaker by facing the issue of deception and fudging without equivocation. In three recent important articles (Rhine, 1973, 1974a, 1974b), he discussed in detail how serious workers in parapsychology have been plagued for many years by the problem of fudging, especially among the new workers in parapsychology.

In his first paper, Rhine (1973) presented several cases of new students who came to the Duke Parapsychology Laboratory and who seemed headed for a career in parapsychology but whose reporting of results was not reliable, which they admitted when faced with the evidence. These students were advised to "seek a career in a less sensitive field" and they concurred.

Rhine (1973) then went on to discuss cases of individuals who had obtained the doctorate in an established field, and who had already reported successful research on ESP. However, the reports presented by individuals in this group at times did not spell out details regarding the usual safeguarding conditions for ESP research. When asked to specify the safeguarding conditions or to improve them, some of the individuals did so and became established researchers but most of the individuals in this category did not do so; in fact, they lost interest in ESP research and did not publish further papers on the topic. In some of these cases "Evidence of altered records led to the suggestion of dishonesty, and when [the individual] was confronted with the evidence, he quickly and quietly dropped all contact with parapsychology" (p. 364.)

Rhine (1973) commented on these cases as follows:

> Yet one must wonder why such a weak and stupid course would be followed, even if rarely, by mature, intelligent, educated individuals already established in much more secure professions than parapsychology. Obviously these [individuals] were not among the strongest and most successful members of their own disciplines. Also, in their superficial view of psi research they probably received a false conception of how easy it would be to gain quick notoriety and advancement in it. The field is of course open to anyone, with almost no checks and balances until a report is submitted. The more accepted rules and standards of psi research are not much in evidence especially to outsiders, and other fields do not raise the strict questions regarding significance, controls, and confirmation that parapsychology editors do. So a would-be experimenter who is of course new to the strictures of this branch of science would naturally be quite surprised if his test results should not reveal the psi effects he had anticipated. Since he

knows that positive results were supposed to be there, he might be tempted to 'top-off' the data to round out the expected result which he has been led to assume. After all, he may easily suspect that this is the way data are 'topped off' and 'rounded out' in many other professions and disciplines, that nobody will be the worse for it, and that plenty of others are probably doing it.

Other pressures too may support him in his attitude. [He] may strongly wish to have a paper accepted for publication or for a convention program, either to help his status or his vanity, or both. The worldwide public attention which has been given to parapsychology has admittedly been the envy of some of the people in other less popular fields. Odd as it may seem, an almost fanatic urge to share in this sort of fame takes hold of some individuals. (pp. 364-365)

In his second paper, Rhine (1974b) discussed a dozen cases "to illustrate fairly typically the problem of experimenter unreliability prevalent in the 1940's and 1950's" (p. 104). With regard to these twelve individuals, "four of them were caught 'red-handed' in having falsified their results; four others did not contest (i.e., tacitly admitted) the implications that something was wrong with their reports that seemed hard to explain and they did not try. In the case of the remaining four the evidence was more circumstantial, but it seemed to our staff they were in much the same doubtful category as the other eight" (p. 104).

Rhine (1974b) stated that during the past 20 years there has been a marked reduction in this type of chicanery, primarily because such risky personnel have been avoided and because steps have been taken to make it very difficult for "dishonesty to be implemented inside the well-organized psi laboratory today" (p. 105). Despite these precautions, a case of dishonesty was discovered soon after Rhine wrote the above words in March, 1974. In June, 1974, Rhine (1974a) wrote as follows in his third paper:

When I wrote my paper on deception for the March issue of the *Journal [of Parapsychology]* I had not expected to come back to the subject again in publication. I thought experimental parapsychology was heading into a stage of successful avoidance of the problems of experimenter dishonesty. Accordingly, I was shocked to discover, only a few months later, a clear example of this same problem, not only right here at the Institute for Parapsychology, but even involving an able and respected colleague and trusted friend. (p. 215)

In this case, a suspicious research assistant concealed himself during the experiment and observed the behavior of Walter J. Levy,

Jr., who was a major investigator in parapsychology. While he was secretly observed, Levy improperly altered the data. When Rhine confronted Levy with the observations of the research assistant, Levy acknowledged that he had fudged the data of the experiment and resigned from the staff of the Institute for Parapsychology. Levy stated that he had fudged the data of the experiment he was conducting because, contrary to his previous experiments, the results were at a chance level and he wanted to bring the results up to a significant level so that others would be stimulated to replicate his previous significant studies. Rhine (1974a) concluded from this case of fudging, along the lines of his earlier articles (Rhine, 1973, 1974b), that (a) "the necessity of trusting the experimenter's personal accuracy or honesty must be avoided as far as possible," (b) a method that can help avoid reliance on the investigator's honesty is to involve a number of investigators in each study and, (c) "each new experiment must be considered in effect only a pilot project until it is eventually repeated by others; and if an important finding is at stake, the more repetitions, the better" (p. 220).

Other Recent Cases

Although outright fraud (fudging of all the data), of the kind that anthropologists discovered with regard to Piltdown man (Jastrow, 1935; MacDougall, 1958; Tullock, 1966), appears to be very rare in scientific research, every once in a while a case is reported of scientists who were caught fudging some of their data. For instance, not too long ago, papers that were published in prestigeful journals (*Science* and *Journal of Infectious Diseases*) were shown to contain fraudulent data (DuShane, Krauskopf, Lerner, Morse, Steinbach, Strauss, & Tatum, 1961).

Fudging of data was also recently demonstrated among physician-researchers who were paid by pharmaceutical companies to evaluate the effectiveness of new drugs. In 1967 a committee from the Food and Drug Administration investigated the validity of the physicians' reports. About one-third of the physicians who were investigated (16 of 50) were found to have supplied fabricated data on the new drugs to the sponsoring drug companies and to the government (N.W., 1973).

Serious questions have also been raised recently with regard to Sir Cyril Burt's results which have been used to support the genetic viewpoint in the recent controversy pertaining to inheritance of intelligence. Kamin (1973) made some surprising discoveries when he looked closely at Burt's data pertaining to IQ in monozygotic twins reared apart. In 1955 Burt reported that he had tested 21 sets of twins, in 1958 he reported that he had tested over 30, and in 1966 he reported that the number tested had reached 53. In each of these three papers, Burt reported that the correlation between the IQs of the twins was .771. It appears almost certain that some part of the data that were reported over the years was incorrect. Either Burt's sample did not increase as he reported or the IQ did not remain perfectly constant (to three decimal places) with an increasing sample from 21, to 30, to 53 pairs of twins. The probability of obtaining three identical correlations is so astronomically small that it seems appropriate to conclude that Burt was either extremely careless in reporting his data or misreported them.

Relevant to the above is the evidence indicating that "cheating" is the norm in a variety of situations and that honesty is present only when individuals are clearly aware that the odds are high that they will be discovered and punished for dishonesty. For instance, in a study with three sociology classes, Tittle and Rowe (1973) ascertained how many students cheated when they were allowed to score their own examinations. They found that only 5 of 107 students totally refrained from cheating during the entire quarter and they concluded that "conformity to the norm of honesty in the classroom situation is unlikely in the absence of control efforts by the instructor" (p. 496). We may deduce from these findings that stronger sanctions are necessary in education and also in science to prevent dishonesty. Let us now turn to some of the motivations that may underlie dishonest reporting of data.

MOTIVATIONS FOR FUDGING

As Reif (1961) pointed out, there is often intense competition among investigators deriving from a variety of factors which cause them to strive for prestige. Investigators commonly invest much time and effort in their research and they are not always neutral with respect to the results they obtain. Some investigators prefer that the results come out a certain way. Beck (1961) noted that, since investigators usually have a vested interest in the successful outcome of their research and feel the pressure to succeed or to blaze new trails, such biases generate error "and—let's face it, since science is done behind closed doors—dishonesty" (p. 219). After noting cases of fraud in science, Beck noted that:

What dishonesty exists among scientists is rarely on such a grand scale. It is subtle and, no doubt, frequently unconscious behavior. The experiments that 'work' are reported with no mention of those that failed. The data that support the hypothesis are seized upon; the rest are explained away or forgotten. (p. 220)

Hagstrom (1965) presented evidence that scientists are motivated to receive recognition, that this motivation influences the types of problems they tackle, and that scientists deny this motivation. Along similar lines, Glaser (1964) noted that the structure of science, which gives rise to competition for recognition, commonly gives rise to feelings of "comparative failure." Scientists who feel they have not received sufficient recognition, may indulge in deviant practices, such as "falsifying, plagiarizing, 'trimming off' bits of inconvenient data, selecting only those data that support one's hypothesis, and reporting only successful results" (Glaser, 1964, pp. 99-100).

The strong drive for recognition and fame among scientists was thoroughly documented by Watson (1968) in his book, which also described how the structure of DNA was discovered. The drive for fame has been present from the very beginning of science. Merton (1969) carefully documented the fact that Darwin, Faraday, Freud, Newton, and many other great scientists struggled and fought to receive recognition for priority of scientific discoveries and that the drive for priority is imbedded deeply in the scientific norm for originality. Merton (1957) also noted that the emphasis on originality in science has in some instances led to fraud, to fudging of data, to plagiarism and to one scientist slandering another. However, Merton also emphasized that the strong norm for honesty in science makes such cases rather rare.

The intense competition among scientists for fame, prestige, and credit for discoveries is widely documented. For instance, a physicist at the University of California recently sued two other physicists at the same university who had been awarded the Nobel prize for the discovery of the anti-proton. The suing physicist claimed that he had originated the seminal idea, designed an experiment to test it, and then revealed the design to the other two physicists. He also claimed that the latter two physicists did the experiment themselves, cut him out of participation, never gave him credit for his idea, and prevented him from doing anything about it for many years by threatening that if he did, they would deny him access to important equipment (the Bevatron) which was necessary for the conduct of his research (Anonymous, 1972b).

In brief, the striving for prestige or visibility among scientists can lead to bias since some investigators seem to believe that whether or not they report significant results can make a difference in their prestige, fame, or career. An investigator may believe, for instance, that if he reports nonsignificant results, he will not be able to publish the report, he will not receive a research grant, or, if he is a doctoral candidate, he will not be granted the doctoral degree. Given this type of motivation to obtain significant results, it can be expected that some investigators may, for example, change one digit of a p value of, say, .15, to a p value of .05.

Since the hypothetical investigator discussed in the above paragraph is aware that he is violating a basic canon of scientific research—namely, to report the results correctly—, he may attempt to rationalize his fudging to himself by arguing that the effect is actually there or that the results are "significant" even though they do not reach an acceptable level of significance. He may rationalize to himself that reporting a $p = .05$ for his results is actually more representative of his data than reporting a nonsignificant $p = .15$.

MOTIVATIONS FOR HONESTY

As implied above, we might expect an Investigator Fudging Effect to occur at times when there is strong motivation to obtain certain results. However, as C.P. Snow (1961) has noted, the motivation to fudge which may be present under these conditions is strongly counterbalanced by a very strong motivation to adhere to the basic canon of research by reporting the results correctly. The motivation to report the results correctly is also strong since the investigator knows that if he is caught fudging his data, he will immediately be expelled from the fraternity of scientists and, if he is even suspected of fudging, he will be treated as a pariah by his colleagues. Tullock (1966) pointed out that the strongest reason why fudging is not more common in the natural sciences is that "fakery is almost certain to be detected, and the probability of detection is highly correlated with the importance of the result reported" (p. 134). Similarly, McCain and Segal (1969) have argued that "An additional restraint is that science, being public in nature, allows checking of data by uncommitted peers" (p. 117). Although the comments by Tullock (1966) and by McCain and Segal (1969) may be valid when applied to the natural sciences, it is questionable to what extent they are also applicable to the behavioral sciences. Since experiments in the natural sciences can often be replicated and cross-validated, fakery can usually be detected. However, since experiments in the behavioral sciences are very difficult to replicate and cross-validate, fakery is much more difficult to detect. If an investigator in the behavioral sciences is unable to cross-validate an earlier study, the author of the earlier study will very likely argue that there were some important differences in the procedure which led to the failure to replicate.

The motivation to adhere to the canons of scientific research is probably sufficient to prevent falsification of data on a "grand scale" in behavioral research. It is open to question, however, whether these canons are also strong enough to prevent "small scale" fudging in which the investigator alters his data or his statistics just enough to "round off the edges," to make his results more "acceptable" (for journal publication or for his colleagues) or to more closely fit the theory to which he is committed. In brief, although the conscience of the investigator and the consequences of being caught are sufficiently strong to prevent "large scale" fudging and probably to prevent "small scale" fudging in the overwhelming number of cases, it might also be expected that, in a few cases, the countermotivation to fudge, which derives from the investment in and the importance of obtaining certain results, finally wins out.

EXPERIMENTER EFFECTS

In the preceding chapters we discussed the pitfalls in research that are associated with the investigator. Before we now turn to the pitfalls associated with the experimenter, we should re-emphasize two points:

1. Even though the same person may be both an investigator and an experimenter, the two roles are functionally quite different. In much present-day research, investigators are highly paid professionals who design, analyze, interpret, and report studies, whereas, experimenters are often graduate or undergraduate students who test the subjects while having only a peripheral involvement in the overall planning of the study.

2. One of the major contentions of this text is that the bias that has often been attributed to the lowly experimenter who runs the study is at times actually due to the high status investigator who has major responsibility for the study. Recent books pertaining to the

pitfalls or artifacts in experimental research (Adair, 1973; Friedman, 1967; Jung, 1971; A.G. Miller, 1972; Rosenthal, 1966; Rosenthal & Rosnow, 1969) have overemphasized the pitfalls associated with the experimenter and have tended to downplay the many pitfalls that are associated with the investigator. In the previous chapters we tried to correct this imbalance by pinpointing some of the many ways that investigators influence the results of their studies. Let us now turn to the role of the experimenter and note some of the ways that he may affect the results.

Pitfall VI
Experimenter Personal Attributes Effect

In a large number of studies, specific personal attributes of the experimenters affected the performance of subjects. For instance, the experimenter's race has at times affected the subjects' responses (Hyman, 1954; Summers & Hammonds, 1965). Similarly, in a host of studies reviewed by a number of investigators (Friedman, 1967, Chapter 6; R.F.Q. Johnson, 1976; Masling, 1960, 1966; Rosenthal, 1966, Chapters 4 and 5), experimenters differing in such characteristics as sex, age, ethnic identity, prestige, anxiety, friendliness, dominance, and warmth at times obtained divergent results when testing similar subjects. In fact, an Experimenter Personal Attributes Effect has been found on a wide variety of tasks including intelligence tests, projective tests, verbal conditioning tasks, and other physiological and educational measures.

Although many studies indicated that an attribute of the experimenter affected the subjects' responses *on the specific task* used in that study, very few studies have been conducted which attempted to determine either (a) whether an attribute of the experimenter, for example, his race, affects subjects' responses on a wide variety of tasks or (b) whether more than one attribute of experimenters, for example, their race, age, and sex, affect subjects' responses on one kind of task, for instance, an intelligence test. Also, the results of studies in this area are now so complex that it is difficult to draw simple conclusions pertaining to the effects of specific experimenter attributes on specifc experimental tasks.

The complex results in this area are illustrated in an interesting paper by Kessel and K.J. Barber (1968). These writers reviewed seven studies which attempted to determine if the effectiveness of an experimenter in producing verbal conditioning in his subjects was related to the experimenter's prestige. They reported the following: three studies found that prestigeful experimenters were more successful at conditioning subjects than non-prestigeful experimenters; two studies found no relationship between experimenter's prestige and subjects' responsiveness; and the remaining two studies showed that non-prestigeful experimenters were more effective in producing verbal conditioning. These complex results do not support the notion that the prestige of the experimenter has a clear-cut, predictable effect even in one type of experiment (verbal conditioning). In fact, as R.F.Q. Johnson (1976) has pointed out, these complex results indicate one or more of the following: "(a) there are extraneous variables confounding the data, (b) the status or prestige of the experimenter interacts in a complex manner with some yet-to-be-determined variable or variables to affect the subjects' behavior, (c) the procedures of these studies are not sufficiently comparable and (d) there is no such 'experimenter prestige effect' in verbal conditioning experiments."

Similar complexity has been found in assessing the effects of other experimenter attributes, for example, race. Hyman (1954), Summers and Hammonds (1965), and other investigators presented data indicating that subjects interviewed by black experimenters give different responses to questions about racial prejudice than those interviewed by white experimenters. However, other investigators have presented data indicating that the effect of the experimenter's race is not found in some studies (Sattler, Skenderian, & Passen, 1972), or is found only under very restricted conditions (Sattler, 1974, p. 32; Sudman & Bradburn, 1974).

Rosenthal (1966, p. 61) noted an important problem in studies which ostensibly demonstrated an Experimenter Personal Attributes Effect: we cannot be certain the effect was due to the observed attribute of the experimenter rather than to a correlated variable. For instance, there is evidence to indicate that female experimenters tend to treat subjects differently from male experimenters. Consequently, "It could be this behavioral variation more than the variation of physical attributes that accounts for the effects on subjects' responses" (Rosenthal, 1966, p. 61).

R.F.Q. Johnson (1976) has pointed out three additional major deficiences in studies which attempted to demonstrate an Experimenter Personal Attributes Effect: (a) They failed to control for the confounding effects of other experimenter attributes. (b) They failed to take into account numerous interactive effects and thus obscured the complex nature of this effect. (c) They failed to use a representative sample of psychological tasks on which to test the hypothesized effects of the experimenters' attributes. Let us now summarize Johnson's (1976) comments with regard to each of these three deficiencies.[1]

FAILURE TO CONTROL FOR OTHER ATTRIBUTES

Although many studies indicate that the results may depend on some characteristic of the experimenter, very few studies have isolated which of the many attributes of the experimenter make a difference and which are insignificant. For example, a study by Binder, McConnell, and Sjoholm (1957) has been often cited as demonstrating the Experimenter Personal Attributes Effect. In this study, on verbal conditioning, whenever the subject used a hostile word, the experimenter reinforced the subject by saying "good." Binder et al. reported that "an attractive, soft spoken, reserved young lady [experimenter] who was five feet and one-half inch in height and 90 pounds in weight" obtained more verbal conditioning from the subjects than an older male experimenter who was "very masculine, six feet five inches tall, 220 pounds in weight, and had many of the unrestrained personality characteristics which might be expected of a former marine captain." Reviewers of this study have attributed the difference in learning rates of the subjects either to the difference in the sex of the two experimenters (Friedman, 1967; Kintz, Delprato, Mettee, Persons, & Schappe, 1965; Rosenthal, 1966) or to the difference in their status (Kessel & K.J. Barber, 1968). However, the two experimenters also differed with respect to age, height, weight, tone of voice, personality, etc. To determine whether the sex of the experimenter affects the results, it is necessary to utilize more than one female and more than one male experimenter. Stated more generally, when testing for an Experimenter Personal Attributes Effect, it is necessary to use a representative sample of experimenters.

FAILURE TO ASSESS INTERACTIVE EFFECTS

There is reason to believe that a personal attribute of the experimenter may interact with an attribute of the subject to affect the results. For instance, the race of the experimenters may interact with the race of the subjects; the results obtained by black and white experimenters may depend upon whether their subjects are black or white. Very few studies have been reported which took into consideration both a personal attribute of the experimenter and a personal attribute of the subject. When such studies have been conducted, complex interactive effects were obtained. For instance, Stevenson and Allen (1964) assessed the interaction between the sex of the experimenter and the sex of the subject in a marble-sorting task and found that female subjects tested by female experimenters performed at a higher level than male subjects tested by female experimenters.

Possible interactions between an attribute of the experimenters and an attribute of the subjects have been taken into consideration in a series of studies by Sarason and his coworkers (Sarason, 1962, 1973; Sarason & Minard, 1963; Winkel & Sarason, 1964). For instance, in a study on verbal conditioning in which the experimenters reinforced the subjects' hostile verbs, Sarason (1962) assessed both the hostility of the experimenters and the hostility of the subjects. There was a significant interaction between the hostility scores of the experimenters and of the subjects such that the highest number of hostile responses came from high hostile subjects seen by high hostile experimenters. After reviewing this and related experiments, Rosenthal (1966) appropriately concluded that, "It appears that at least in studies of verbal conditioning, when an experiment is so designed as to permit the assessment of complex interactions, these interactions are forthcoming in abundance. Only rarely, however, are most of them predictable or even interpretable" (p. 43).

In brief, although very few experiments have evaluated the effects of both experimenter characteristics and subject characteristics, it appears likely that complex interactions are present in this area. As Johnson (1976) has pointed out:

> On the basis of existing data, it appears that even though the experimenter's attributes may be readily hypothesized to affect subjects' responses on particular tasks, these "main" effects may actually be part of very complex relationships. For example, what may at first appear to be a simple relationship between the race of the experimenter and white subjects' responses to a race-related questionnaire may actually turn out to be part of a complex interaction with other variables such as the educational level of the subject, the number and nature of prior experiences the subject has had with black people, the social class of the experimenter, the geographical location of the study,

and the historial time period in which the study is conducted . . .
Complex interactive effects, rather than simple main effects, may be
the hallmark of the results of future investigations on the hypothesized
effects of the experimenter's personal attributes.

FAILURE TO SAMPLE PSYCHOLOGICAL TASKS

Almost all studies that assessed the effects of the experimenters'
attributes on subjects' performance, used only one type of task, for
example, a verbal learning task or verbal conditioning (Sarason,
1962). It is questionable whether results obtained with one kind of
task are generalizable to other tasks. Johnson (1976) noted that the
various tasks that could be used can be categorized along four
dimensions:

1. The experimenter is more involved in administering some tasks
and less involved in others for example, the experimenter is more
involved in administering a Rorschach test than a Minnesota
Multiphasic Personality Inventory (MMPI). It can be hypothesized
that the experimenters' characteristics may have a greater effect on
subjects' responses when the task calls for more experimenter
involvement.

2. Some tasks, for example, the Rorschach, the Thematic
Apperception Test (TAT), and Rosenthal's person-perception task,
are more ambiguous than other tasks because the correct or
acceptable response is not clear. Since, with ambiguous tasks, the
subjects tend to search for additional cues or for information on
which to base their response, it can be hypothesized that the more
ambiguous the response, the more likely that the experimenters'
characteristics will affect the subjects' responses.

3. The experimenters' attributes may have different effects
depending on the degree of difficulty of the task. For instance, in
order to impress female experimenters, male subjects may try harder
to show their strength on difficult physical tasks. This difference
may not be detected when the tasks are easy or when the
experimenters are male.

4. It appears that an experimenter's attribute is more likely to
affect the subjects' responses on a task when the attribute "corre-
sponds" with the task. For instance, it appears that the race of the
experimenter is more likely to affect subjects' responses on a
race-related task such as a test of racial prejudice (Hyman, 1954;
Summers & Hammonds, 1965), the sex of the experimenter is more

likely to affect subjects' responses on a sex-related task such as a questionnaire on sexual feelings (Benney, Riesman, & Star, 1956; Walters, Shurley, & Parsons, 1962), and the hostility of the experimenter is more likely to affect subjects' responses on measures of hostility (Sarason, 1962). In fact, there has even been a study indicating that a mustachioed experimenter can affect subjects' performance on drawing tasks—subjects tend to draw more mustachioed men (Yagoda & Wolfson, 1964).

CONCLUSIONS

It appears that all that can be said with confidence at the present time is that an experimenter's sex, age, race, prestige, anxiety, friendliness, dominance, etc. may *at times* affect how subjects perform in the experiment, but we can rarely predict beforehand what experimenter attributes will exert what kind of effects on subjects' performance on what kinds of experimental tasks. Clearly, much further research is needed in this area.

Until further research is conducted, an investigator who wishes to generalize his results broadly should have his study carried out by experimenters who differ on relevant personal attributes. The problem here is to decide beforehand on which relevant attributes the experimenters should differ. Certainly, if the dependent variable is related to race (e.g., attitudes toward segregation), the investigator should use both black and white experimenters. Similarly, if the subjects' responses might be affected by the experimenters' sex, age, prestige, etc., the investigator should use sets of experimenters who differ on these attributes.

Since investigators rarely use a sample of experimenters to conduct their studies, conclusions from studies should be stated more cautiously. The conclusions from studies should include the proviso that the results may be limited to the specific kind of experimenter(s) who was (were) used in the study. Of course, much of the emphasis on cross-validation of experiments in psychology and the social sciences derives from this consideration—namely, that an Experimenter Personal Attributes Effect may have operated in the original study and that the results may not be valid when experimenters with different characteristics conduct the same study.

NOTES

1. I am indebted to Richard F.Q. Johnson for permission to summarize his important paper.

Pitfall VII
Experimenter Failure to Follow
the Procedure Effect

Earlier in this book, we discussed the Investigator Loose Procedure Effect which refers to the *investigator's* failure to construct an experimental protocol that specifies clearly how the experimenter is to conduct the study. There is evidence to indicate that when the investigator does not standardize the procedures and allows the experimenters to vary how they carry out the study, experimenters may conduct the study differently with different subjects and this variability can affect the results (Feldman, Hyman, & Hart, 1951; Page, 1971; Raffetto, 1967).

Let us now assume that the investigator has constructed a tight experimental protocol that does not allow the experimenter much room to vary the procedure. The question now at issue is how often and under what conditions does the *experimenter* fail to follow the standardized experimental procedures? Of course, if the experimenter deviates significantly from the experimental procedures, the study that is published by the investigator is misleading—the study that was actually conducted is not the same as the one that is reported.

Although much has been written during recent years about how the experimenters' expectancies can unintentionally influence their subjects' responses, very little has been said about how the experimenters, by deviating from the prescribed experimental procedures, can lead the investigator to present misleading results. In fact, with very few exceptions, studies that attempted to assess the effects of the experimenters' expectancies simply assumed that the experimenters carried out the procedures in the way they were supposed to. They rarely checked to determine if an Experimenter Failure to Follow the Procedure Effect was present. This important aspect of the research process—implementing the experimental procedures—has been surprisingly neglected.

In an important investigation, Friedman (1967, Chap. 5) attempted to ascertain how experimenters implemented the procedures. The study showed very convincingly that most experimenters have serious difficulties in following the experimental procedures closely even when the experimental protocol is standardized or is not especially "loose." Friedman's data showed that experimenters vary in the way they greet their subjects, in the way they read the instructions, and in the way they implement the specific experimental procedures. For instance, when greeting the subjects, "The extremes are represented by the experimenter who, introducing himself by name, rises and shakes hands with each of his subjects and the seated experimenter with the sour expression whose very first line is 'I am going to read you some instructions' " (Friedman, 1967, p. 75). Not only do experimenters vary in the way they conduct the experiment, but also the same experimenter tends to be inconsistent when testing different subjects. For instance, an unmarried male experimenter typically conducts the experiment somewhat differently when his subject is a pretty, single woman than when his subject is a male. Friedman (1967, p. 104) found that when the subject is female rather than male, male experimenters are more likely to look directly at the subject, to smile when greeting the subject, and to use the subject's name or an affectionate phrase ("dear"). In a wide variety of experiments, female subjects have performed differently from male subjects (Carlson, 1971). Although the differences in performance were attributed to differences in sex, they may have been actually due to the fact that the experimenters (who were almost always males) behaved differently toward their female subjects and their male subjects.

In addition to deviations from the standardized experimental procedures, there appear to be wide deviations in kinesic and vocal behavior on the part of the experimenter (Friedman, 1967). Experimental protocols do not specify how the experimenter is to conduct himself kinesically and vocally. The underlying problem here, as Friedman (1967) noted, is that experiments are not conceptualized within the frame of reference of social interaction and nonverbal communication. Consequently, experimental protocols do not tell the experimenter how he should greet the subject, how the experimenter and the subject should be seated, whether the experimenter should ever look or smile at the subject, how long the experimenter should take to read the instructions, and how the subject should be dismissed (Friedman, 1967, p. 73).

After observing a substantial number of experimenters administering Rosenthal's person-perception task, Friedman (1967) concluded as follows:

> Psychological experiments are supposed to be standardized, controlled, replicable, objective. These experimental sessions were understandardized, uncontrolled, different, heterogenous. Psychological experimenters are supposed to be inflexible, mechanical, 'programmed,' standardized in their behavior. These experimenters improvised and adlibbed and were nonconforming, different, variable in their behavior.
>
> The resemblance between this experiment as observed and the experiment as it is usually reported is at best a likeness between distant relatives in an extended family.
>
> What seem to be standardized are our collective illusions about the 'standardized' experiment and the 'standardized' experimenter. (p. 106)

Although Friedman's data indicate that experimenters *typically* deviate in minor and apparently unimportant ways from the experimental protocol, they also suggest the possibility that some experimenters under some circumstances may deviate more markedly from the specified experimental procedures.

An Experimental Failure to Follow the Procedure Effect has been demonstrated in a rather large number of studies in which subjects were interviewed (Hyman, 1954). These studies found that a substantial proportion of interviewers deviated markedly from the specified procedures; they skipped questions that were to be asked and held discussions with the subject which were not part of the script. In fact, Hansen, Hurwitz, Marks, and Mauldin (1951) and also Kish and Slater (1960) found that interviewers varied the way they asked the questions even when they were told explicitly that they were to stick with precisely worded questions. Furthermore, Cannell and Kahn (1968) suggested that there appears to be a universal tendency for interviewers to introduce flexibility into their interviews. Apparently interviewers must be carefully supervised during training in order to instill in them the importance of following the procedures carefully.

This part of the research process—implementing the experimental procedures—requires much more careful scrutiny. When reinforcing cues or words are not part of the experimental protocol, how often do experimenters reward their subjects for expected or desired responses by smiling or by saying "good", "fine" or "excellent"? Under what conditions do experimenters change the procedures that are listed in the protocol or add new features to the prescribed procedures? Is the experimenter more likely to follow the standardized procedures closely when the results he obtains are harmonious with the investigator's hypothesis and more likely to deviate from the procedures when the results are disconfirming the hypothesis? Very few studies have been conducted on this topic, and further research should prove fruitful.

Pitfall VIII
Experimenter Misrecording Effect

The experimenter may follow the specified experimental procedures and yet may fail to record the subjects' responses correctly. If the errors in recording are systematic (not randomized), they can give rise to invalid results—an Experimenter Misrecording Effect.

Investigators typically assume that their experimenters correctly recorded the subjects' responses and they rarely check to see if the assumption is correct. Although the assumption is probably valid most of the time, there are data indicating that it is incorrect in some circumstances. Laszlo and Rosenthal (1971) found that experimenters made errors in adding their subjects' scores and that 75 percent of the errors were in the direction of the experimenters' expectancies or desires (Rosenthal, 1966, p. 13). More closely related to the Experimenter Misrecording Effect are data presented by Silverman (1968) and Johnson and Ryan (in press) indicating that some experimenters wrongly record their subjects' responses and that these misrecordings are in line with the results that the experimenters' expect or desire. Similarly, O'Leary, Kent, and Kanowitz (1975) found that experimenters' tended to misrecord their subjects' responses in line with the investigators' desires when the investigator was present during the experiment and tried to influence the experimenters' recordings (by commenting on how he perceived the subjects' responses).

Johnson and Adair (1970) reported that some experimenters misrecorded their subjects' responses in line with their (the experimenters') expectancies. In another study utilizing a word-association task, the same investigators (Johnson & Adair, 1972) found that when the stimuli (words) were presented by an automated procedure (by a tape recording) female experimenters obtained results in line with their expectancies or desires by systematically misrecording the data. Johnson and Adair interpreted these results as follows:

> Why, then, did the experimenters, particularly the females, err more with the automated procedures? There seems to be at least three possible explanations, none of which are unequivocal. Operating the tape recorder instead of having to read each stimulus word may have: (1) given these experimenters more freedom to consciously attempt to "fudge" the data; (2) given them more time to 'play' with the timer switch leading to more errors; or (3) caused them to feel a greater need to 'fudge" the data as they had no opportunity to influence their subjects in the way they enunciated the stimulus words. (p. 93)

In brief, the systematic misrecording of data that was present in the above experiment was interpreted by Johnson and Adair in terms of fudging. We shall discuss experimenter fudging in the next section of this text but we shall use the term somewhat differently from Johnson and Adair to refer, not to systematic misrecording per se, but to the experimenter presenting fabricated data to the investigator.

In two more recent experiments which assessed subjects' responses on three tasks (Rosenthal's person-perception task, a marble-dropping task, and a latency-of-word association task), Johnson and Ryan (in press—Experiments 3 and 4) again found that some of the experimenters systematically misrecorded their subjects' responses so as to obtain the results they wanted to obtain.

J.L. Kennedy (1952) reported several studies on ESP in which recording errors by the experimenters accounted for the results that were favorable to ESP. Kennedy appropriately noted that the subjects' guesses in ESP experiments should be recorded either by an investigator who does not know what is the correct answer or by automatic equipment because "human beings . . . are not trustworthy recording devices" (p. 515), especially when they desire particular results. This suggestion, that the person recording the subjects' guesses during ESP tests should not know the correct response, was accepted during the early years of the Duke laboratory and became standard procedure (Rhine, 1974b).

Additional studies are needed to determine how often and under what conditions experimenters systematically misrecord the subjects' responses. Let us now turn to related studies which indicated both that experimenters at times systematically misrecord the subjects' responses and also at times fudge the data *after* they have recorded the subjects' responses.

Pitfall IX
Experimenter Fudging Effect

Previously we discussed the *Investigator* Fudging Effect, which is very difficult to document because the investigator has practically complete control over the original data and can make only selected portions of it available for checking by other investigators. However, fudging on the part of the *experimenter* is not too difficult to document.

Of course, if the experimenter knows that he is being observed, he will not be likely to indulge in fudging. However, it is not too difficult to carry out studies in which the experimenter is not aware that possible fudging on his part is under scrutiny. For instance, some subjects can be used as stooges who give predetermined responses. A check can then be made later to determine if the experimenter's data are in harmony with the subject's responses. This kind of check has been used in a substantial number of studies which involved interviewing of subjects. When such an attempt was made to check fudging in the interview situation, falsification of data was found more often than had been expected (Andreski, 1972, p. 109).

Hyman (1954) has described the study done by the American Jewish Committee in which 15 interviewers were hired for a special interviewing job. Each interviewer was to administer a standard questionnaire to one to four respondents who were actually stooges and who were particularly difficult to interview. For example, one stooge played the role of a hostile bigot—he had been instructed to be hostile, uncooperative and suspicious of the entire situation.

Another stooge played the role of a punctilious liberal—he had been instructed to play the role of an individual who felt incapable of giving an unqualified answer to any question he was asked. Half of the interviewers fudged much of their data and *all* of the interviewers fudged at least some of their data. That is, each of the 15 interviewers at one time or another fudged data either by not asking a question but recording a response anyway or by recording a response when a respondent did not give an answer to the question.

The study described in the preceding paragraph, which involved an especially difficult interview situation, apparently involved more fudging than is usually the case. Wyatt and Campbell (1950) found that 55 percent, 123 of 223, student interviewers either did not complete their interviews or fudged some of their data. Using college students as interviewers, Guest (1947) and Sheatsley (1947) also found some fudging occurring, but apparently to a lesser degree than in the two studies mentioned above.

Roth (1966) presented a series of testimonials from "hired-hand" experimenters who admitted that they had fudged their data. Roth then went on to present cogent arguments why some fudging may be typical among hired-hand experimenters—that is, experimenters who do not feel they have a stake in the research and who feel that they are "simply expected to carry out assigned tasks and turn in results which will 'pass inspection.' "

Roth argued that the behavior of hired-hand experimenters can be expected to be similar to that of a hired hand in a production organization. He described a series of studies which show that, to make their job easier, hired hands in a production unit typically cut corners on prescribed job procedures, fake time sheets, and indulge in other forms of goldbricking. Roth pointed out that the product which the hired hand turns out is not his in any sense—he does not design it or decide how it will be produced or what is to be done with it afterwards. Given this alienation from the work, it can be expected that hired hands (working on a production unit or serving as experimenters) will typically deviate from the prescribed procedures and "cut corners" or fudge data.

Another kind of fudging has been observed in studies which utilized two experimenters to record a specific subject response. In these kinds of studies, the experimenters are typically asked to compute a reliability coefficient which indicates to what extent they agree in their recordings. O'Leary and Kent (1973) found that student experimenters tend to "cheat to obtain high reliabilities." The student experimenters at times improperly communicated with each other when they were making their recordings, at times changed their recordings to inflate the degree of agreement, and at times made computational errors which spuriously inflated the level of agreement.

Azrin, Holz, Ulrich, and Goldiamond (1961) inadvertently discovered that, when an experiment is practically impossible to carry out, a substantial number of experimenters (undergraduate and graduate students) fudge the data. At the beginning of their investigation, Azrin et al. were attempting to determine whether, in a natural nonexperimental setting, the type of statements made by unselected individuals would be influenced by statements made by experimenters. The experimenters were to strike up conversations with individuals in a natural setting and, for a period of time, were to record the number of statements made by the individuals (the subjects) which expressed an opinion. After the base line for opinion statements had been determined, the experimenter was to reinforce the subject's opinion statements by agreeing with them, *to say nothing more*, and to record how many statements the subject subsequently made during a specified period of time which expressed an opinion. The aim of the study was to determine whether individuals would increase the number of their statements which stated an opinion if the experimenters reinforced their opinion statements by agreeing with them.

In one of these studies, Azrin et al. found that when four sophisticated investigators (presumably the authors themselves) tried to conduct the experiment, the experiment could *not* be conducted in accordance with the specified experimental procedures because all individuals who were approached broke off the conversation within a short period when the experimenter simply agreed with their opinions and refused to say anything more.

In another study in this series, 16 graduate students were asked to carry out the same experiment. Of the 16 experimenters, 15 reported that they completed the experiment successfully and 14 presented data which seemed to indicate that their subjects proffered more opinions after their opinions had been reinforced. However, one experimenter stated that he was unable to conduct the experiment because he was unable to maintain a conversation with his subjects without actively participating in the conversation. Subsequently eight of the remaining experimenters admitted that they also had similar difficulties and that they had deviated appreciably from the experimental procedures. Clearly, in this part of the investigation at least half of the experimenters showed an

Experimenter Failure to Follow the Procedure Effect. Some of these experimenters may also have fudged part or all of their data, as indicated by a third study reported by Azrin et al. (1961).

In this third study, Azrin et al. asked undergraduate students to carry out the same experiment. Again, the experimenters reported that they had succeeded in carrying out the study and their data indicated that reinforcement had influenced the subjects to give more opinions. However, much of the data had been fudged. Azrin et al. (1961) discovered the fudging as follows:

> By coincidence, a student was enrolled in this third class who was also employed as a research assistant in a psychology laboratory. This student employee was assigned to question the other students informally and outside of class as to how they had conducted their experiments. The other students had no knowledge of this arrangement. Out of 19 students questioned, consisting of almost one-half of the class, 12 stated that they fabricated part or all of the data. This admission . . . was readily made when the student was asked by the employee, 'I'm having trouble with my experiment; can you tell me how you did yours?' Five of the remaining seven students questioned stated that they had deviated greatly from the prescribed procedure. Only two out of nineteen students stated that they had followed the prescribed procedure. Consequently, an attempt at an exact replication seemed pointless, since the data reports themselves were probably fabricated. (p. 29)

In brief, the studies by Azrin et al. indicated that when an experiment is practically impossible to conduct according to the specified experimental procedure, a substantial proportion of experimenters (undergraduate or graduate students) carry out the impossible study either by changing the experimental procedures (Experimenter Failure to Follow the Procedure Effect) or by fabricating the data (Experimenter Fudging Effect).

Of course, additional investigations are needed to determine how often and under what conditions experimenters fail to follow the prescribed experimental procedures, misrecord the data, or fudge the data.

Pitfall X
Experimenter Unintentional Expectancy Effect

Experimenters commonly *expect* certain results; for instance, they expect that the experimental group will perform differently from the control group. Experimenters also commonly *desire* certain results, for example, they would like to see the experimental hypothesis verified. In the 1960's, Rosenthal (1963, 1964a, 1964b, 1966) hypothesized that (a) the experimenters' expectancies or desires are transmitted to their subjects by means of *unintentional* paralinguistic cues (such as variations in the experimenter's tone of voice) or *unintentional* kinesic cues (such as changes in the experimenter's posture or facial expressions), and (b) the experimenters' expectancies or desires influence (or bias) *their subjects' responses*, that is, the subjects respond in such a way as to confirm the experimenters' expectancies or desires—Experimenter Unintentional Expectancy (or Desire) Effect.

A rather large number of studies have been conducted which attempted to demonstrate the Experimenter Unintentional Expectancy (or Desire) Effect.[1] Most of these studies failed to show the effect, that is, they failed to show that the experimenters' expectancies affected the subjects' responses. Paradoxically, instead of showing an Experimenter Unintentional Expectancy Effect, some of these studies seemed to show either an Investigator Data Analysis Effect, an Experimenter Failure to Follow the Procedure Effect, and Experimenter Misrecording Effect, or an Experimenter Fudging Effect. A small number of these studies, however, indicated that the experimenters' expectancies can significantly influence the subjects' responses.

This chapter, which will review the studies pertaining to the Experimenter Unintentional Expectancy Effect, will be longer and more detailed than the preceding chapters in this text. The complexity of this chapter is due to the following: (a) during recent years, the Experimenter Unintentional Expectancy Effect has received more publicity and far more attention from psychologists than all of the other pitfalls in research combined, (b) a large number of studies have been conducted which pertain to this effect, (c) investigators who claimed to have demonstrated the effect did not avoid the pitfalls that have been discussed previously in this book and, consequently, (d) studies which pertain to the Experimenter Unintentional Expectancy Effect can serve to illustrate some of the many pitfalls in research.

The organization of this chapter is as follows. First, I shall analyze an illustrative study which claimed to show an Experimenter Unintentional Expectancy Effect but which can be interpreted as showing an Investigator Data Analysis Effect. Next, I shall summarize studies which were interpreted as showing an Experimenter Unintentional Expectancy Effect but which can be interpreted as illustrating an Experimenter Failure to Follow the Procedure Effect, an Experimenter Misrecording Effect, or an Experimenter Fudging Effect. Following these discussions I shall review 75 studies conducted in recent years which attempted to demonstrate the Experimenter Unintentional Expectancy Effect. This review will show that (a) most studies either failed to demonstrate the effect or obtained equivocal results, (b) in some studies experimenters obtained results in line with their expectancies by varying how they conducted the experiment or how they scored the subjects' responses, and (c) a few studies showed an Experimenter Unintentional Expectancy Effect either as a main effect or in interaction with other variables.

EXPERIMENTER UNINTENTIONAL EXPECTANCY EFFECT OR INVESTIGATOR DATA ANALYSIS EFFECT?

Several years ago Barber and Silver (1968a, 1968b) critically reviewed 31 studies which purported to show an Experimenter Unintentional Expectancy Effect. Ironically, most of these studies seemed to show an Investigator Data Analysis Effect on the part of those investigators who were seeking to demonstrate the Experimenter Unintentional Expectancy Effect. I analyzed two of these studies (Rosenthal, Persinger, Mulry, Vikan-Kline, & Grothe, 1964b; Rosenthal, Persinger, Vikan-Kline, & Multry, 1963) previously when I discussed the Investigator Data Analysis Effect (Pitfall IV.). Let us look at an additional study by Persinger (1963) which was concerned with the Experimenter Unintentional Expectancy Effect but which, paradoxically, seemed to show, instead, an Investigator Data Analysis Effect.

In this study (Persinger, 1963), as in most of the studies that attempted to demonstrate an Experimenter Unintentional Expectancy Effect, student-experimenters were asked to test subjects on Rosenthal's person-perception task. When using this task, the student-experimenter shows the subjects a series of photographed faces. The subject is asked to rate on a numerical scale whether each of the persons shown on the photographs has been experiencing success (high ratings) or has been experiencing failure (low ratings). Preliminary studies had shown that the photographed faces are actually neutral or ambiguous, that is, the neutral faces on the photographs are difficult to rate as having experienced either success or failure.

Twelve student-experimenters participated in this study by Persinger (1963). Six of the student-experimenters were given reasons by the investigator why they should expect that their subjects would give high ("success") ratings on the person-perception task, and the remaining six experimenters were given reasons to expect that their subjects would give low ("failure") ratings. Persinger hypothesized that the experimenters' expectancies would affect the ratings of those subjects with whom they were previously acquainted significantly more than those subjects with whom they were not acquainted. To test this hypothesis Persinger performed three different statistical analyses. These analyses yielded non-significant findings. After the investigator (Persinger) had failed to confirm his original hypothesis in three separate analyses, he changed the hypothesis. The revised hypothesis was that there is an interaction between the experimenters' expectancies, the sex of the experimenters, and whether or not they are acquainted with their subjects. The investigator performed two statistical analyses to test this revised hypothesis. One of the two analyses did not show the hypothesized interaction. The other analysis showed a significant interaction which indicated that the expectancies of male experimenters (but not of female experimenters) affected their acquainted subjects more than their unacquainted subjects.

The last statistical analysis mentioned above was presented as a definitive finding—as showing that an Experimenter Unintentional Expectancy Effect had been demonstrated in interaction with the other variables (Rosenthal, 1968). However, this conclusion is invalid. The study did not show an interaction between experimenters' expectancies and other variables because it is based on an Investigator Data Analysis Effect. It should be noted that the investigator did not confirm his original hypothesis in three separate analyses; he went on to perform two analyses which pertained to a revised hypothesis, and one of the latter two analyses did not confirm the revised hypothesis. These kinds of analyses lead to misleading conclusions. If investigators keep changing their hypothesis and perform several statistical analyses on each hypothesis, sooner or later they will obtain a "significant" finding even when the data come from a Table of Random Numbers.[2]

EXPERIMENTER EXPECTANCY, FAILURE TO FOLLOW THE PROCEDURE, MISRECORDING, OR FUDGING?

Two studies (Rosenthal & Fode, 1963a, Rosenthal & Lawson, 1964) were interpreted by their authors as indicating that experimenters' expectancies unintentionally influence the performance of rats. Although these studies have been widely quoted as indicating that the Experimenter Unintentional Expectancy Effect is found even when experimenters are testing animals, the results are open to a different interpretation, namely, that the studies showed one or more of the following: An Experimenter Failure to Follow the Procedure Effect, an Experimenter Misrecording Effect, or an Experimenter Fudging Effect.

In both of these studies, the experimenters were undergraduate students enrolled in a beginners' psychology laboratory course. The experimenters were told by the investigator that they would receive practice in duplicating well-established experimental findings pertaining to rats. Half of the experimenters were told (falsely) that their rats came from a bright strain and would learn quickly and the other experimenters were told that their rats came from a dull strain and would learn slowly. (The rats were actually drawn at random from a homogeneous animal colony and thus were equal in brightness.) In both studies the experimenters expecting fast learning from their rats reported significantly faster learning than the experimenters expecting that their rats were slow learners. Rosenthal (1966) interpreted this outcome as showing that the experimenters' expectancies unintentionally influenced the rats' responses. Rosenthal further hypothesized that experimenters expecting faster learning handled their rats differently from those expecting slower learning and that the tactual cues transmitted during handling mediated the Experimenter Unintentional Expectancy Effect.

However, there are alternative interpretations of these studies. As stated above, the experimenters were undergraduate students enrolled in a beginners' psychology laboratory. Students in introductory laboratory courses deviate from the standardized experimental procedures and systematically misrecord the data to such an extent that most psychologists agree that the results from such laboratories cannot be trusted. In fact, the authors of these studies reported that failure to follow the experimental procedures and misrecording or fudging of data were occurring in their laboratories. In the Rosenthal and Fode (1963a) study, the student experimenters were rarely observed by the laboratory supervisor; however, during the brief period in which they were observed, there were "five observed instances of cheating in which an E prodded an S [a rat] to run the maze" (p. 186). However, Rosenthal and Fode did not consider this type of cheating or failure to follow the specified procedures—prodding the rats to run the maze faster—especially important because it was not observed more often among experimenters expecting faster learning from their rats.

Regarding the second study (Rosenthal & Lawson, 1964), one of the investigators subsequently stated (without presenting further details) that "several instances of data fabrication came to light" (Rosenthal, 1964a, p. 83). We can, of course, assume that the investigators did not use the data that they knew were fabricated. However, there is no way of knowing whether the remaining student experimenters in the introductory laboratory course who were not caught in the act of fudging the data and whose data were used in the analysis conducted the study honestly or dishonestly.

In brief, although these studies have been widely cited as showing that an Experimenter Unintentional Expectancy Effect is present even when the experimenters are testing rats, there is presumptive evidence that the results were due, not to an Experimenter Unintentional Expectancy Effect, but to an Experimenter Failure to Follow the Procedure Effect, an Experimenter Misrecording Effect, or an Experimenter Fudging Effect. Additional studies are needed to determine which of these kinds of effects play the most important role in biasing the results of experiments conducted in introductory laboratory courses.[3]

STUDIES THAT FAILED TO FIND AN EXPERIMENTER UNINTENTIONAL EXPECTANCY EFFECT

A series of studies reviewed in detail by Barber and Silver (1968a, 1968b) failed to find an Experimenter Unintentional Expectancy Effect. For instance, Barber, Calverley, Forgione, McPeake, Chaves, and Bowen (1969) presented five studies which failed to demonstrate that experimenters' expectancies affect subjects' responses on Rosenthal's person-perception task. Similarly, McFall (1966), Wartenberg-Ekren (1962), White (1962) and others reported that experimenters did *not* obtain results in line with their expectancies.

At least 40 studies which were conducted subsequent to the reviews by Barber and Silver (1968a, 1968b) (or which were not available when Barber and Silver wrote their reviews) also failed to find an Experimenter Unintentional Expectancy Effect. Let us briefly summarize these studies.

Three experiments conducted by Souren, van der Kloot, and van Bergen (1969), single experiments reported by Bootzin (1971), Bloom and Tesser (1971), Hawthorne (1972), Perlmutter (1971),[4] and Compton (1970),[5] and six additional experiments (Freedman, 1970; Hertzog & Walker, 1973; Jacob, 1968; McFall & Saxman, 1968; McGinley, McGinley, & Murray, 1972; Wessler & Strauss, 1968) used Rosenthal's procedures with his person-perception task and failed to replicate his original findings: experimenters who were led to expect high ("success") ratings on the person-perception task obtained the same ratings as those led to expect low ("failure") ratings.

In two experiments, Johnson and Ryan (in press, Exps. I and II) failed to find an Experimenter Unintentional Expectancy Effect on Rosenthal's person-perception task and on a word association task. However, in both experiments, there was evidence to indicate that about half of the experimenters were either suspicious of the expectancy manipulation or did not understand or failed to remember what they were supposed to expect. Apparently, what occurred in these experiments can be labeled as a Failure of Experimental Manipulation Effect.

In their third and fourth experiments, the above cited authors (Johnson & Ryan, in press) attempted to ascertain whether experimenters could bias their subjects' responses when they deliberately tried to do so. The experimenters were asked to attempt deliberately to elicit certain kinds of responses from their subjects by means of nonverbal and paralinguistic cues, that is, without telling their subjects directly how to respond. In both experiments, the experimenters were unable to influence the way their subjects responded (on Rosenthal's person-perception task, on a marble-dropping task, and on a latency-of-word association task). Although the experimenters did not significantly influence their subjects' responses, there was evidence in both experiments that some of the experimenters misrecorded the data systematically in the direction of the results they were trying to obtain.

A series of studies utilizing the Wechsler Intelligence Scale for Children (WISC) also failed to find an Experimenter Unintentional Expectancy Effect. In a study by Saunders and Vitro (1971), 60 second-and third-grade children were tested on the WISC by six examiners from the graduate program in either clinical psychology or counseling. The examiners were told (falsely) that the teachers considered some of the children as gifted and others as retarded and they were to be tested to justify placing the children in the special programs for gifted or retarded. The examiners reported IQ scores that did not differ for the "gifted" or "retarded." In fact, two of the six examiners requested special conferences to report that the teachers' assessments of "gifted" and "retarded" were markedly inaccurate. Additional investigations (Blatchley, 1970; Dangel, 1970, 1972; Gillingham, 1970) also failed to show that experimenters' expectancies affected subjects' responses to the Wechsler intelligence scales for children or adults.

A series of recent studies which assessed subjects' responses on other kinds of tasks also failed to find the effect. Martuza (1971) failed to find an Experimenter Unintentional Expectancy Effect in a study in which the subjects were asked to guess the outcomes of coin tosses while the experimenters were led to expect that some subjects would guess more "head" outcomes than other subjects.[6] Zegers (1968) and Kennedy (1969) failed to find the effect in experiments on verbal conditioning. Another study indicated that experimenters' expectancies did *not* affect the results of the experiment although the experimenters *believed* (wrongly) that their results were harmonious with their expectancies (Kent, O'Leary, Diament, & Dietz, 1974). Other studies which measured subjects' responses to a variety of experimental tasks also failed to show the Experimenter Unintentional Expectancy Effect (Beasley & Manning, 1973; Becker, 1968; Dana & Dana, 1969; Hipskind & Rintelman, 1969; Jacob, 1970, 1971; Janssen, 1973; Landon, 1972, McGinley, McGinley, & Shames, 1970; Steinhelber, 1970; Strauss, 1968; Strauss & Marwit, 1970; Timaeus & Lueck, 1968b; Wessler, 1968, 1969; Yarom, 1971).

The 40 recent experiments cited above indicate that it is rather difficult to demonstrate an Experimenter Unintentional Expectancy Effect. This should not be surprising. It should be emphasized that in the above studies the investigators tried to transmit expectancies to the experimenters and then hoped that the experimenters would in turn transmit their expectancies to the subjects and that the subjects would respond in accordance with the experimenters' expectancies. Consequently, for the above studies to have shown an Experimenter Unintentional Expectancy Effect, it was necessary for a seven-step transmission process to have taken place successfully (cf., McGuire, 1968): 1) The experimenter had to attend to the expectancy communication from the investigator. 2) The experimenter had to comprehend the expectancy communication. 3) The experimenter had to retain the communication. 4) The experimenter had to unintentionally emit cues which were capable of informing the subject of his (the experimenter's) expectancy. 5) The subject had to attend to the cues from the experimenter. 6) The subject (consciously or unconsciously) had to comprehend what the cues from the experimenter meant. 7) The subject (intentionally or unintentionally) had to alter his responses so that they confirmed the experimenter's expectancy. The transmission chain could have broken down at any one of these seven links. In the studies which have been conducted, the investigator told the experimenter what results were expected quite some time before the experimenter tested the subjects. At the same time, the investigator also told the experimenter many other things besides what to expect—for example, he told the experimenter how to obtain and how to test the subjects. When the experimenter was told what to expect, he may not have paid close attention or may not have understood the communication. Furthermore, by the time the experimenter ran his subjects he may have forgotten what results were expected. When the experimenter ran his subjects, he may have failed to emit cues which informed the subject of the expected results. Even if the experimenter emitted such unintentional cues, the subject may not have noted them or, if he noticed them, he may not have understood what they meant. Finally, even if the subject understood what the experimenter expected, he may not have altered his responses to fulfill the experimenter's expectancy. Instead, the subject may simply have responded in his normal manner (not altering his responses) or may have altered his responses so as to disconfirm the experimenter's expectancy—the "Screw You Effect" (Masling, 1966).

In fact, a thorough review by Weber and Cook (1972) found very little evidence that experimental subjects typically try to respond in accordance with the experimenter's expectancies or try to confirm what they believe is the experimenter's hypothesis which they deduce from cues ("demand characteristics") in the experimental situation (Orne, 1962).[7] Instead, subjects in experimental situations, in the same way as individuals in most social situations, typically try to put their best foot forward, that is, they try to appear competent, normal, likeable, etc. Their concern with how they will be judged ("evaluation apprehension") is far more important than their concern about fulfilling the experimenters' expectancies or confirming his hypothesis. Although, at times, the subjects' desire to "look good" may induce them to respond in accordance with the experimenters' expectancies, it appears that more commonly their desire to appear competent, normal, etc., induces them to respond naturally without being influenced by the experimenters' expectancies. In addition to the many studies summarized by Weber and Cook (1972), other studies also support the above contentions. For instance, in an experiment on verbal conditioning (Koenigsberg, 1971), only about one-third of the subjects who were aware that the experimenter was trying to produce verbal conditioning were "motivated to comply", that is, tried to do what was expected or desired. Of the remaining subjects, most tried to respond naturally without being influenced by the experimenters' expectancies or hypotheses and a few were "motivated not to comply", that is, they resisted responding in accordance with the experimenters' expectancies.

STUDIES WITH EQUIVOCAL RESULTS

Six recent studies that tried to demonstrate an Experimenter Unintentional Expectancy Effect gave rise either to equivocal results that are open to a variety of interpretations or to results that were opposite to the experimenters' expectancies. Let us summarize these studies.

Using Rosenthal's person-perception task, Mayo (1972) found that, overall, the experimenters' expectancies did not affect the subjects' responses. However, Mayo's study included two sets of experimenters: one set was not observed during the experiment and the second set of experimenters knew they were being observed. The experimenters who were not watched obtained results more in line with their expectancies than the experimenters who knew they were being observed.

Using Rosenthal's standard procedures, Adler (1973) found that experimenters led to expect high or low ratings on the person-perception task did not differ in the results they obtained. However, Adler's study included another group of experimenters who were led to expect high or low ratings on the person-perception task and, in addition, were told that the study was being conducted to confirm previous results and that it was *necessary* for them to confirm the previous findings before moving on to the next phase of the research. This part of the study showed that when experimenters are told that it is necessary to obtain certain results, they are able to do so. Unfortunately, no data were provided as to how these experimenters obtained the results they were told they had to obtain.[8]

Barko (1970) also obtained ambiguous results while following Rosenthal's standard procedures with the person-perception task: experimenters expecting medium ratings obtained lower ratings than those expecting low or high ratings. In another study using Rosenthal's procedures with the person-perception task, the subjects run during the first half of the experiment were not affected by the experimenters' expectancies but the subjects run during the last half of the experiment gave ratings that were *opposite* to the experimenters' expectancies (Uno, Frager, Takashima, Scherer, & Rosenthal, 1970). Unfortunately, the same researchers failed to replicate their results in a later study (Uno, 1974). However, results *opposite* to the experimenters' expectancies have also been obtained in a study on verbal conditioning (Koenigsberg, 1971).

"CONFIRMING" EXPECTANCIES BY VARYING THE CONDUCT OF THE EXPERIMENT

Earlier studies (e.g., Masling, 1965), reviewed by Barber and Silver (1968a, 1968b), suggested that the experimenters expectancies may affect the way the experimenter conducts the experiment and may give rise to an Experimenter Failure to Follow the Procedure Effect. Two recent experiments (Hersh, 1971; Page, 1971); also indicate that experimenters can obtain the results they expect (or desire) by varying the way they conduct the experiment.

Page (1971) reported that when experimenters expected their subjects to be responsive to verbal conditioning, they did not obtain more verbal conditioning (as compared to control subjects), but when they expected that their subjects would not be responsive to verbal conditioning, they obtained significantly less verbal conditioning. These results were due in part to the fact that the experimenters treated those subjects from whom they did not expect conditioning somewhat perfunctorily: the experimental interactions did not last as long with such subjects as compared to subjects from whom the experimenters expected conditioning.

Hersh (1971) found that experimenters' expectancies significantly affected results with children on the Stanford-Binet Intelligence Scale and that this effect was due, at least in part, to the following: when the referral information stated that the children were high rather than low on intellectual ability, the experimenters began testing the children on the Stanford-Binet at a higher year level.

EXPECTANCY AND EXPERIMENTERS' SCORING OF RESPONSES

Earlier studies (e.g., Laszlo & Rosenthal, 1967; Silverman, 1968), reviewed by Barber and Silver (1968a, 1968b), suggest that the experimenters' expectancies may influence the manner in which they judge and score the subjects' responses. Recent studies by Johnson and Adair also indicate that experimenters' expectancies may lead to an Experimenter Misrecording Effect.

Johnson and Adair (1970) found that (a) experimenters' expectancies affected the outcome of a study utilizing a word-association task and (b) the effect was due primarily to the experimenters' expectancies affecting how they observed and recorded their subjects' responses. In a later study which also used a word-association task, the same authors (Johnson & Adair, 1972) did not find an overall expectancy effect but a significant interaction indicated that female experimenters at times obtained results in line with their expectancies by systematically misrecording the data.

Eight recent studies indicate that, when the experimental task is ambiguous, that is, when it is unclear as to how it is to be scored or what is a correct response, the experimenters' expectancies can affect how they (the experimenters) interpret or score their subjects' responses. This kind of effect can occur, for example, in administering certain subtests on intelligence scales which require the experimenter or examiner to interpret the subjects' responses before assigning a score (Sattler, 1974, p. 61). A representative study along these lines was presented by Egeland (1969) who asked inexperienced examiners to score selected responses given by children to three subtests of the Wechsler Intelligence Scale for Children—the Comprehension, Similarities, and Vocabulary subtests. The responses that were selected were ambiguous and difficult to score. Some of the examiners were told that the ambiguous responses came from above-average children while other examiners were told that they came from below-average children. The examiners' expectancies significantly affected their scoring of the ambiguous responses from the Comprehension and Similarities subtests. Other investigators (Babad, Mann, & Mar-Hayim, 1975; Sattler, Hillix, & Neher, 1970; Schroeder & Kleinsasser, 1972; Simon, 1969) similarly found that experimenters' expectancies affected their scoring of ambiguous responses on certain subtests of the Wechsler Intelligence Scales.

Additional studies have also shown that experimenters' interpretation or scoring of ambiguous or difficult-to-score responses can be influenced by their expectancies. These ambiguous responses included the distance between the heads of two individuals who were observed on videotape (Johnson & Ryan, in press), the amount of "eye contact" between pairs of interacting subjects (White, Hegarty, & Beasley, 1970), the degree of pupil dilation on photographed faces (Bell, 1971), and the "effectiveness of psychotherapy" as judged from audiotapes of two interviews conducted with a patient at the beginning and end of his psychotherapy (Tinstman, 1970).

STUDIES INDICATING AN EXPERIMENTER UNINTENTIONAL EXPECTANCY EFFECT

In some of the studies summarized above, the experimenters' expectancies affected either the manner in which the experimenters judged or scored the subjects' responses or the way the experimenters conducted the experiment. Although these studies indicate that experimenters' expectancies can affect the outcome of the experiment by affecting the *experimenters* judgements or procedures, they do not demonstrate an Experimenter Unintentional Expectancy Effect ("Rosenthal Effect"), that is, they do not demonstrate that experimenters' expectancies are unintentionally transmitted to the subjects and the *subjects* then respond so as to fulfill the experimenters' expectancies. However, several earlier studies (e.g., Adair & Epstein, 1968; Marwit & Marcia, 1967; Rosenthal & Fode, 1963b, Exps. 1 and 2; Shames & Adair, 1967), reviewed by Barber and Silver (1968a, 1968b) and Rosenthal (1968), suggested that experimenters' expectancies may unintentionally influence *the subjects' responses*. Ten recent studies, described below, also indicate that experimenters' expectancies may be unintentionally transmitted to subjects and subjects may respond in accordance with the experimenters' expectancies. Although the studies described below suggest an Experimenter Unintentional Expectancy Effect, there are two reasons why it is difficult to conclude that they conclusively demonstrate the effect: (a) It is at times difficult to determine whether the experimenters' expectancies actually affected *the subjects' responses*. (Although the results were in line with the experimenters' expectancies this may at times have been due to changes in the way the experimenter scored the subjects' responses, the way he conducted the experiment, etc.). (b) Even if the experimenters' expectancies affected the subjects' responses, we do not know whether the experimenters' expectancies or desires were transmitted to the subject unintentionally or *intentionally*. (If the experimenter *intentionally* transmitted his expectancies or desires to the subject, the results could more easily be attributed to an Experimenter Failure to Follow the Procedure Effect rather than an Experimenter Unintentional Expectancy Effect.) I shall return to these kinds of issues later, after I have summarized the relevant studies.

Irving (1969) and Blake and Heslin (1971) reported that experimenters' expectancies significantly affected the subjects' ratings on a person-perception task. Also using Rosenthal's standard procedures and his person-perception task, Page (1972) found the following: (a) When mental patients served as experimenters and other mental patients served as subjects, the experimenters' expectancies did not affect the results. (b) When nurses served as experimenters and mental patients served as subjects, a significant effect was obtained in the reverse direction, that is, experimenters expecting high ratings obtained lower ratings than experimenters expecting low ratings. (c) When alcoholic experimenters tested alcoholic subjects, experimenters obtained results which were significantly in line with their expectancies. Timaeus and Lueck (1968a) similarly reported an involved experiment that indicated that experimenters at times obtained results in line with their expectancies.[9]

In each of the studies described above, the authors concluded that the experimenters' expectancies had unintentionally affected the subjects' responses. Although this interpretation is reasonable, it is not imperative—the effects of the experimenters' expectancies on the results may have been mediated in other ways, for instance, by affecting how the experimenters conducted the experiment. Similar considerations apply to other studies that concluded that an Experimenter Unintentional Expectancy Effect had been demonstrated. For instance, in a study by Kennedy, Cook, and Brewer (1970) subjects were more responsive to verbal conditioning when the experimenters expected their subjects to be responsive rather than unresponsive. How the experimenters' expectancies affected the results of this experiment is not clear. When the experimenters expected conditioning, as opposed to when they did not expect conditioning, they may have administered the reinforcements and other aspects of the experimental procedure differently (Experimenter Failure to Follow the Procedure Effect), they may have recorded the data differently (Experimenter Misrecording Effect), or they may have unintentionally transmitted cues which influenced the subjects' responses ("Rosenthal Effect" or Experimenter Unintentional Expectancy Effect).

An additional series of recent studies, however, has presented stronger evidence indicating an Experimenter Unintentional Expectancy Effect. Zobel and Lehman (1969) found that experimenters' expectancies can influence the subjects' responses on a tone discrimination task and presented suggestive evidence that the expectancy effect can be mediated (probably unintentionally) by either verbal or facial cues from the experimenter. McFall and Schenkein (1970) showed that experimenters expectancies can be transmitted by verbal cues and can influence the responses of some types of subjects (subjects who are high in need for achievement and in field dependence). Other studies (e.g., R.W. Johnson, 1970; Marwit, 1969; Miller, 1970) also indicated that the experimenters' expectancies or desires can be communicated to their subjects by verbal, facial, or gestural cues and that the subjects may then respond in such a way as to fulfill the experimenters' expectancies.[10]

EXPERIMENTER EXPECTANCY AS AN INTERACTIVE EFFECT

Recent experiments (Minor, 1970; Smith & Flenning, 1971; Todd, 1971), which used Rosenthal's procedure and his person-perception task, indicated that experimenters' expectancies affect the results with some types of subjects but not others. Minor (1970) showed that experimenters' expectancies affected the responses of subjects only when high "evaluation apprehension" was induced, that is, when the subjects were told that poor performance on their part would indicate that they were psychologically maladjusted. Smith and Flenning (1971) found that experimenters' expectancies affected the responses of subjects who were high in need for approval, and Todd (1971) reported that experimenters' expectancies affected the performance of children who were oriented towards social evaluation and were responsive to social cues. Also working with children but utilizing a marble-dropping task, Dusek (1971) showed that the experimenters' expectancies affected the results obtained with girls but not boys.[11]

Two further studies obtained an interaction between experimenters' expectancies and ambiguity of the experimental task. Shames (1971) found that experimenters' expectancies affected the results only when the subjects were required to make ambiguous judgments (to judge the "color richness" of colors). Similarly, Felton (1970) found that experimenters' expectancies had a greater effect on the subjects' responses when the subjects were asked to rate highly ambiguous photographs rather than photographs that could be rated without difficulty. Felton noted that, when the task was highly ambiguous, the experimenters were aware that their subjects looked to them for assistance as to how to respond or for reinforcement of their responses.[12]

SUMMARY AND CONCLUSIONS

Let us now summarize and draw conclusions from the many studies that have been concerned with the Experimenter Unintentional Expectancy Effect.

1. A substantial number of earlier studies which aimed to demonstrate an Experimenter Unintentional Expectancy Effect had serious defects in data analysis. Paradoxically, the Investigator Data Analysis Effect appears to be at least as common in studies concerned with "experimenter bias" as in any other area of psychological research. It is strongly recommended that the training of behavioral scientists should include greater emphasis on the problems in data analysis that were discussed in this text under Pitfall IV.

2. Two earlier studies were interpreted by their authors as indicating that experimenters' expectancies unintentionally influence the performance of rats. However, these studies, which were conducted by undergraduate students in their introductory psychology laboratory, are open to alternative interpretations, namely,

that the students "biased" their results by deviating from the experimental protocol (Experimenter Failure to Follow the Procedure Effect), by misrecording data (Experimenter Misrecording Effect), or, possibly, by fabricating data (Experimenter Fudging Effect). It is strongly recommended that (a) investigators should *not* assume that experiments carried out by students in the introductory psychology laboratory are conducted in accordance with the experimental protocol and are free of misrecording and fudging and (b) much more emphasis should be placed in introductory psychology laboratories in conducting experiments according to the prescribed procedures and reporting them honestly.

3. At least 40 recent experiments (published since 1968) reported that the experimenters' expectancies did *not* affect the results. In addition, six recent studies either obtained equivocal results, which did not clearly support the hypothesized Experimenter Unintentional Expectancy Effect, or obtained results opposite to the experimenters' expectancies. It thus appears that the hypothesis that experimenters obtain results in line with their expectancies is much more difficult to demonstrate than was implied in a series of earlier reviews (Friedman, 1967; Kintz, Delprato, Mettee, Persons, & Schappe, 1965; Rosenthal, 1963, 1964a, 1964b, 1966, 1967, 1968, 1969). Although in recent years, the Experimenter Unintentional Expectancy Effect has received more attention in the writings of behavioral scientists than all of the other pitfalls in research combined, it is strongly recommended that researchers should be concerned at least as much with each of the other nine pitfalls that are discussed in the present text as they have been with the Experimenter Unintentional Expectancy Effect.

4. There is evidence to indicate that, when the experimental procedures are not strictly defined and the experimenters can conduct the experiment somewhat differently with different subjects, experimenters can obtain expected (or desired) results by varying how they conduct the experiment. The recommendation here is that investigators should be careful to standardize the experimental procedures, that is, they should avoid an Investigator Loose Procedure Effect. For example, when data from an experimental interview are used as dependent variables, the interview should be standardized and conducted in the same way for each subject, preferably by written (instead of oral) questionnaire.

5. The experimenters' expectancies (or desires) can affect how the experimenters interpret or score the subjects' responses, *especially when the criteria for scoring are ambiguous*. It is strongly

recommended that investigators either not use ambiguous tasks or else take special pains to clarify for experimenters exactly how the responses are to be scored.

6. Ten recent studies provided suggestive evidence that experimenters' expectancies can be transmitted to subjects by facial or postural cues and can affect the *subjects' responses*. Also, five recent studies indicated that experimenters' expectancies can influence the responses of some types of subjects but not others and two studies indicated that experimenters' expectancies can influence the responses of subjects when the subjects are asked to respond to ambiguous stimuli. Although these studies did not clearly demonstrate that the experimenters *unintentionally* affected the subjects' responses, they did demonstrate that experimenters' expectancies can influence the performance of at least some subjects. The conclusion here is that experiments should more often utilize "blind" experimenters, that is, experimenters who do not know the experimental hypothesis or experimenters who assess the subjects' responses without knowing what experimental treatments the subjects have received.

NOTES

1. Henceforth, we shall refer to the Experimenter Unintentional Expectancy Effect instead of to the Experimenter Unintentional Expectancy (or Desire) Effect. However, the reader should keep in mind that, in practically all of the experiments that will be discussed below, the experimenters' expectancies were not separated from their desires.

2. A rather large number of additional studies which aimed to show an Experimenter Unintentional Expectancy Effect can be interpreted as showing an Investigator Data Analysis Effect (instead of an Experimenter Unintentional Expectancy Effect). Two of these studies were discussed in detail earlier in this text (Pitfall IV) and others (e.g., Friedman, 1967; Marcia, 1961; Pflugrath, 1962; Rosenthal & Fode, 1963b, Exp. 3; Rosenthal, Friedman, Johnson, Fode, Schill, White, & Vikan, 1964; Rosenthal, Friedman, & Kurland, 1966; Rosenthall, Kohn, Greenfield, & Carota, 1965; Rosenthal, Persinger, Mulry, Vikan-Kline, & Grothe, 1964a; Rosenthal, Persinger, Vikan-Kline, & Fode, 1963) are discussed in detail by Barber and Silver (1968a, 1968b) and Rosenthal (1968).

3. Two additional earlier studies with planaria (Cordaro & Ison, 1963) and rats (Ingraham & Harrington, 1966) indicated that expectancies can affect the way undergraduate student-experimenters judge and score ambiguous or difficult-to-score responses by the animals. Consequently, further studies in this area should also pay careful attention to clarifying for the student-experimenters what criteria they are to use to score the animal's response.

4. When investigators fail to demonstrate an Experimenter Unintentional Expectancy Effect, they at times go on to perform post-mortem analyses of the data in an apparent effort to show that the effect is present in some complex or subtle way. These post-mortem analyses usually give rise either to uninterpretable results or to an Investigator Data Analysis Effect. To illustrate these contentions, I shall comment briefly on the four studies mentioned above by Bootzin (1971), Bloom and Tesser (1971), Hawthorne (1972), and Perlmutter (1971).

Bootzin (1971) failed to confirm Rosenthal's basic findings in two studies—the experimenters did not obtain results in line with their induced expectancies. In both studies, however, the experimenters also recorded how they themselves expected each subject would perform (stated expectancies). These stated expectancies were made after the experimenters were told (by the investigator) what to expect and after they met each subject. In the first experiment, but not in the second experiment, the experimenters' stated expectancies were related to their subjects' performance. In the second experiment, however, there was a significant interaction (Days X Experimenters' Stated Expectancy) indicating that on the third day of the experiment, the experimenters obtained results in the *opposite* direction from what they said they expected. What the latter interaction means is unclear. It is also not clear why Bootzin analyzed his results separately by days. The latter analysis may involve an Investigator Data Analysis Effect, that is, the data are cut in extraneous ways, for example, by days (or time of day or other imaginable ways) and further analyses are performed which provide additional chances to obtain some "significant" effect. It is clear, however, that the results obtained by Bootzin on the third day of his first and second experiment are contradictory and that no conclusions can be drawn from these data.

In the Bloom and Tesser (1971) study, half of the subjects had been forewarned of the possibility of experimenter bias. Since forewarning was expected to reduce the impact of experimenters' expectancies, Bloom and Tesser predicted a significant Forewarning X Expectancy interaction. The predicted interaction was not obtained. Bloom and Tesser then dropped one-third of their subjects, performed an additional post-mortem statistical analysis and reported that now a triple interaction (Sex X Forewarning X Expectancy) was marginally significant ($p < .10$). It appears that the additional post-morten analysis was inappropriate and that this study can be considered under the pitfall that I have previously labeled as the Investigator Data Analysis Effect.

After having failed to demonstrate that the experimenters' expectancies influenced their results, Hawthorne (1972) carried out post-mortem statistical analyses and obtained a difficult-to-interpret interaction indicating that experimenters who were told that they would be paid at a high rate for their work biased their male subjects (but not their female subjects) more than experimenters who were told that they would be paid at a low rate.

After having failed to find an Experimenter Unintentional Expectancy Effect, Perlmutter (1971) performed further statistical analyses which suggested that the experimeneters' expectancies may have had some slight effect. However, Perlmutter admitted that he was "straining for statistical significance" (p. 7) and finally concluded that "even under optimal experimental conditions, expectancy effect magnitudes as assessed by the Rosenthal Person Perception task are at best low and marginal" (p. 94).

5. Compton (1970) also obtained ambiguous results with a reaction time task.

6. Martuza also assessed how confident the subjects were in their guesses and found a significant effect that may have been related in a very complex and indirect way to the experimenters' expectancies. The latter very complex effect reported by Martuza is interesting in that it is one of the most uninterpretable findings that the present author has ever seen. Martuza himself appropriately stated that his interpretation of the significant finding "is highly speculative and further research is necessary before any firm conclusions can be drawn" (p. 170).

7. Orne (1962) argued that experimental subjects typically adopt the role of the "good subject", that is, they try to contribute to knowledge by providing data which are useful to the experimenter and to science. In taking the role of the "good subject" they commonly desire to confirm the experimenter's hypothesis. Orne further stated that subjects try to discover the hypothesis from information available to them—statements made when they were recruited for the experiment, pre-experimental "scuttlebutt", experimental instructions and procedures, experimental tasks, etc. Orne (1962) labeled the totality of such cues which reveal the experimenter's hypothesis as the "demand characteristics" of the experimental situation. The reader should consult the papers by Orne (1962, 1969) for further discussion of these topics.

8. Gallo and Dale (1968) also demonstrated that experimenters can influence their subjects to give more cooperative or competitive responses on the prisoner's dilemma game if they *deliberately* try to do so by indicating approval for the responses they desire and disapproval for the responses they do not want.

9. The experimenters in this study could be subdivided into four sets. One-tailed *t* tests were performed on each of the four slices of data and one of the four *t* tests was significant, indicating that one of the four sets of experimenters obtained results in line with their expectancies.

10. Additional studies, which did not manipulate the experimenters' expectancies but instead manipulated how the experimenters behaved during the instruction-reading period, indicated that subjects can be induced to rate more of the photographed individuals on Rosenthal's person-perception task as having experienced success (high scores) if (a) the experimenters emphasize the word *success* when they are reading the instructions (Duncan, Rosenberg, & Finkelstein, 1969; Duncan & Rosenthal, 1968; Scherer, Rosenthal, & Koivumaki, 1972) or (b) the experimenters maintain a great deal of eye contact with the subjects during the instruction period (Jones & Cooper, 1971).

11. In a follow-up investigation, Dusek (1972) found that the experimenters' expectancies affected the results only when the experimenters expected better performance from girls and the girls were low on test anxiety.

12. After the Experimenter Unintentional Expectancy Effect had been widely publicized by Rosenthal and had become a rather "hot" and somewhat faddish research area, a series of published papers referred to this topic in their title and in their discussion but they did not actually test the effects of experimenters' expectancies (Dickstein & Kephart, 1972; Goebel & Stewart, 1971; V.S. Johnson, 1970; McCaa, 1971; P.A. Miller, 1972; Ohler, 1971; Weiss, 1969). Other studies (Marwit & Strauss, 1975; Thalhofer, 1969) have also been published which seem to pertain to the effects of experimenters' expectancies but the reports are so ambiguous that they are difficult to evaluate. Also, a study by Sheehan (1969) seemed to indicate that experimenters' expectancies affected the outcome in a study on verbal conditioning; however, a follow-up study by the same investigator (Sheehan, 1970) showed that the results of the earlier study were *not* due to the experimenters' expectancies.

Overview and Recommendations

Since experimental research is carried out by fallible individuals, it is open to a wide variety of pitfalls. In the preceding chapters, I have focused on two sets of pitfalls, one set that is associated with the investigator (who designs, supervises and has major responsibility for analyzing and reporting the study) and another set that is associated with the experimenter (who tests the subjects and collects the data).

Recent books and papers in this area have heavily emphasized one of the pitfalls that is associated with the experimenter (the Experimenter Unintentional Expectancy Effect or "Rosenthal Effect") and they have tended to downplay the important role of the investigator. However, we need to become sensitized to the bias that is introduced by the investigator as well as the bias that is associated with the experimenter. Experimental studies are biased at their very outset by the investigator's paradigm and associated theories—by his underlying assumptions and his way of conceptualizing the area of inquiry (Investigator Paradigm Effect). Investigators also design the experiment and construct the experimental protocol and both the specific experimental design and the "looseness" or "tightness" of the specified experimental procedures can exert an important influence on the experimental outcome (Investigator Experimental Design Effect and Investigator Loose Procedure Effect). Investigators also sometimes analyze their data in such a way that they obtain the results they desire or expect (Investigator Data Analysis Effect).

Finally, some investigators are highly motivated to report certain results and, despite the scientific canon to present the results honestly, fabrication of some of the data may at times occur (Investigator Fudging Effect).

Present-day experimenters (who are often graduate or under-graduate students) can also bias the results of the research. At times the experimenter's personal attributes—his sex, age, race, prestige and personality characteristics—can affect the way his subjects perform in the experiment (Experimenter Personal Attributes Effect). Experimenters sometimes deviate from the experimental protocol and carry out an experiment which differs from the one that was planned and reported by the investigator (Experimenter Failure to Follow the Procedure Effect). Also, some experimenters systematically mis-record their data (Experimenter Misrecording Effect) and a few experimenters may fabricate some of their data (Experimenter Fudging Effect). Finally, the experimenter's expectancies or desires are at times unintentionally communicated to the subjects, and the subjects sometimes alter their responses so as to confirm the experimenter's expectancies or desires (Experimenter Unintentional Expectancy Effect).

Experimental research can become a more reliable method for obtaining valid knowledge if the following changes are instituted.[1]

1. Investigators should become more aware of their underlying paradigms and how paradigms influence every aspect of their research (Kuhn, 1962). Investigators should also try to make their assumptions (which derive from their underlying paradigms and associated theories) more explicit (cf. Barber, 1970b; Chaves, 1968; Spanos, 1970; Spanos & Chaves, 1970).

2. At the present time the same investigator who plans the study also has major responsibility for analyzing the data. Research studies would be less biased if the investigator who plans the study and who has an investment in the outcome is *not* the same person who has responsibility for the data analysis.

3. At times the same person plans the study (serves as investigator) and also collects the data (serves as experimenter). It is recommended that the investigator who plans the study and who has a strong commitment to the outcome should *not* be the same person who serves as experimenter and who collects the data.

4. Although it is advisable for investigators not to serve as experimenters, they should more often serve as "pilot" subjects in their own studies. In this way, they may gain insight into how the subjects view the experimental design, may be able to "tighten" the

design, and may change experimental instructions that are not clear to the subjects. Also, as Carlson (1971) pointed out, if investigators do not administer to subjects those treatments they do not wish to "take" themselves and administer only those they have "taken" themselves, it would elevate the ethical standards of research—the researcher may be more prone to accept "the responsibility for his own choices and for the consequences of these choices" (p. 216). Also, researchers who serve as "pilot" subjects in their own studies may discard tendencies to impose unnecessary testing programs or exhaustive experimental manipulations.

5. Investigators should become more sensitive to the importance of the experimental script or protocol. A "loose" protocol that does not clearly specify how the experimenter is to carry out each phase of the study and that fails to consider the various contingencies that may arise can easily yield misleading results.

6. Investigators should give their experimenters more supervised practice in implementing the experimental protocol and in correctly and honestly recording the data. Before the formal experiment is conducted, the experimenters should carry out pilot studies under careful supervision.

7. In the training of researchers, additional emphasis should be placed on the complexities of data analysis. Researchers need to have a thorough understanding of many kinds of data analyses that lead to misleading conclusions and the kinds of analyses that can be used appropriately with specified sets of data (cf. Barber & Silver, 1968a, 1968b; Elashoff & Snow, 1971).

8. The emphasis on "positive" results in graduate schools and in the training of researchers needs to be changed. Research should be judged on the validity of the design and procedures that are used to answer the questions that are posed rather than on the outcome or the results that are obtained (Rosenthal, 1966).

9. The present training ground for psychologists, the intro-ductory psychology laboratory, is permeated with improper pro-cedures—failing to follow the experimental protocol, misrecording of data and fudging of data—and this early "training" may influence the investigator's later attitude toward the collection of data. Teachers of embryo psychologists and educators should place much more emphasis on the value of carefully following the prescribed proce-dures and carefully and honestly recording the data.

10. Investigators should check, much more often than they do at present, to see if their experimenters are faithfully implementing the experimental protocol and are carefully and honestly recording the

data. This check could be made in various ways—by making tape recordings or video tapes of the experimenters carrying out the study, by using one-way mirrors to observe the conduct of the experiment, or by sending stooges, who give predetermined responses, to be tested by the experimenters.

11. Investigators should more often use sets of experimenters differing in personal attributes to collect the data. Too often experiments are carried out by one experimenter and the results may be influenced by the characteristics of that one experimenter.

12. More often than at present, experiments could be carried out "blind" (the data collector does not know what treatment the subject has received), the experimenter administering the experimental procedures could be a different person from the one who records the results, subjects could be given written or tape-recorded instructions, and automated equipment could be used both to administer the experimental procedures and to record the results (Rosenthal, 1966).

13. There are so many pitfalls in any one experimental study that we should not take any one study too seriously. Before they are accepted as an integral part of the area of inquiry, the results of any experiment should be replicated by independent investigators. As Plutchik (1968) has stated: "Rather than rely exclusively on statistical tests to confirm the reality of an obtained effect, researchers should rely more on independent replication of results . . . 'One replication is worth a thousand t-tests' " (p. 119). The importance of replication has not been sufficiently emphasized. For instance, Bauernfeind (1968) noted that only 1 of 10 textbooks on educational research included *replication* in its index.

Although *exact* replications are rare in the behavioral sciences (Denzin, 1970, p. 32; Sterling, 1959), partial replications or non-exact replications are not uncommon. In the latter case, subsequent studies attempt to identify the conditions under which the initial findings are valid and they commonly include either a non-exact replication of the original experimental conditions or their conceptual equivalent (Ostrom, 1971). As Lykken (1968) has pointed out, there is a need in psychology for "constructive replications," that is, more investigators should attempt to confirm empirical relationships that were claimed in earlier reports while the replicator formulates his own methods of sampling, measurement, and statistical analysis.

However, we also need more "operational replications" in which an attempt is made to duplicate exactly the "Methods" section of an earlier report. Since this type of replication tends to conflict with the scientific norm for originality, it is rarely rewarded, and thus is quite uncommon (Boalt, 1969). The replication of an earlier study would be a very worthwhile and profitable activity for the beginning researcher (Ary, Jacobs, & Asghar, 1972; Borg & Gall, 1971; Thompson, 1974). A method for encouraging "operational replications" has been elucidated by Raney (1970). He suggests that psychology departments should encourage the graduate student to carry out a replication study for his master's thesis. Raney notes that it is questionable whether most master's theses makes a contribution to the field. Replication studies would guarantee scientific significance to the master's thesis without loss to the student since, in order to choose and defend the thesis, he must still acquire knowledge of a field and research skills.

POSTSCRIPT: THE FUTURE OF EXPERIMENTAL RESEARCH

Before this text was mailed to the publisher, it was read critically by nine young researchers or graduate students.[2] After completing the text, three of the readers felt that, since there were so many problems in experimental research, it may be wiser to forsake experimentation in general (and laboratory experiments in particular) and to limit our knowledge-seeking attempts to other methods, for example, to naturalistic field studies or to participant observation.

Some established investigators who have studied the pitfalls in experimental research have arrived at similar conclusions as the readers mentioned above. For example, Silverman (1970) has argued that the best way to avoid the many problems of experimental research is to conduct fewer studies in the laboratory and more in natural settings:

> The best way to make a person not behave as a Psychological Subject is not to let him know he is one.
> The direction of unobtrusive methods in natural setting has, in perspective, much to recommend it. Since our beginnings, psychologists have brought people to experiments rather than experiments to people, and it has become an assumption almost as unquestioned as treatments and controls. Students planning their first experiment ask almost reflexively, 'Where is my laboratory room?' and, 'Where do I get my subjects?'. Perhaps they should be taught to ask, 'Where is the behavior I want to study going on?' and, 'How do I test my theories about it while keeping it reasonably intact?'. We may have fewer studies, but we will probably have sturdier laws of behavior. (p. 721)

Although studies conducted in natural settings are useful, and certainly more of them should be conducted, this does not solve the problems of research (Cooper, 1974). Many of the pitfalls in research that we discuss in this book also apply to studies carried out in natural settings, even when unobtrusive measures are used. As Fromkin and Streufert (1973) have pointed out, "Identification of laboratory 'artifacts' provides only false security for research conducted in 'natural settings' because the same 'artifacts' are found to operate in a wide variety of nonlaboratory settings (cf. Argyris, 1952, 1968; Dunnette & Heneman, 1956; Kroger, 1967; Page & Lumia, 1968; Rosen, 1970; Rosen & Sales, 1966; Roethlisberger & Dickson, 1946; Scott, 1962)."

It needs to be underscored that experimental studies are useful even though they are not attempting to duplicate a real life situation. Festinger (1953) appropriately emphasized that if one wants to study a real life situation, he should go directly to the real life situation. However, experiments serve other purposes and have several major advantages. For instance, they provide an opportunity for *systematic* variation of the variable which is hypothesized to produce a particular effect, they provide an opportunity to assign subjects *at random* to the various treatments, and, since other variables can be "controlled," they have the potential to specify unambiguously that changes in one variable X causes changes in variable Y (Fromkin & Streufert, 1973).

Stated somewhat differently, experiments are conducted to determine the relationship between theoretically-defined variables when an attempt is made to isolate the variables and they thus have their own purposes. The experimenter tests a hypothesized relationship between variables by *manipulating* the independent variable. In real-life situations we are rarely able to manipulate the independent variable and observe its effect on the dependent variable. As Wuebben, Straits, and Schulman (1974) pointed out:

> ... ideally everything that takes place in an experiment is controlled by the experimenter who sets up the situation in such a way that the results of the study will be maximally useful in testing causal relationships among the variables of interest. Thus from the scientist's point of view the experiment is particularly attractive *because* it is contrived, *because* it is artificial, and *because* it is therefore devoid of all the confounding variables that exist in the real world. (p. 16)

Other important aspects of experimental research have been delineated by Kelman (1968). He writes that "experimental research can make enormously important contributions to social-psychological knowledge. These contributions, however, take the form of providing *unique inputs into systematic thinking about social-psychological processes*, rather than of establishing laws about social behavior" (p. 159). Kelman pointed out that systematic thinking about man and society is the essential task of the social psychologist. He then delineated four ways in which experimental research is very useful in the process of thinking about social behavior. First, by translating concepts into experimental operations, the social psychologist begins to discover ambiguities that he had not previously noticed and is forced to face difficulties that he had avoided. In fact, by constructing an experiment, the social psychologist is forced to commit himself, to state what his concepts mean, and to specify exactly what relationships he expects.

Second, experiments can show that postulated causal relationships *can* occur, at least under certain circumstances. Thirdly, experimental situations allow the psychologist to study the relationships between his variables in a detailed fashion while other variables are controlled. Finally, experimental studies provide data that stimulate further thinking especially when the experimental findings are not anticipated. Kelman concluded that, *"An experimental finding, at least in our field, cannot very meaningfully stand by itself. Its contribution to knowledge hinges on the conceptual thinking that has produced it and into which it is subsequently fed back."* (p. 161).

In brief, experiments are useful as *one* method of attaining knowledge. Other methods of inquiry—e.g., naturalistic field observations, participant observation, survey research, cross-cultural analysis,—are, of course, also useful. In fact, I wholeheartedly agree with Levine (1974) that "methodologists in psychology [should] distinguish between problems that can be studied by experimentation and those that cannot and [should] stop insisting that all problems are better handled with the logic of experimental design and statistical inference" (p. 664).

In summary, although there are many pitfalls in experiments, experimental research will continue to be conducted in the behavioral sciences because it is a useful, heuristic method of inquiry. However, researchers should become more sensitized to the many pitfalls in experimental studies that have been outlined in this text. The underlying theme of the text has been that the validity and generalizability of experiments can be significantly improved by making more explicit the pitfalls that are integral to their planning and execution, by emphasizing these pitfalls in the training of graduate students, and by keeping the pitfalls in full view of researchers who conduct experimental studies. I hope that the present text, by focusing more attention on the pitfalls, will play a role in improving the planning, conduct, analysis, and interpretation of experiments.

NOTES

1. Rosenthal (1966, Chapters 17-24) has also suggested a series of changes that should be made in the methods of experimental research. Although Rosenthal's discussion is concerned primarily with techniques for controlling the Experimenter Unintentional Expectancy Effect (and tends to downplay the many other investigator and experimenter effects that have been discussed in the present chapter), it is nevertheless stimulating and well worth careful reading. I am incorporating some of Rosenthal's suggestions into the 13 recommendations that I am listing here.

2. I am deeply indebted to R.F.Q. Johnson for stimulating discussions concerning the contents of this text, for his critical readings of the manuscript, and for his invaluable assistance in drafting the section on Pitfall VI (Experimenter Personal Attributes Effect). I am also grateful to Marla Lynch and Marjorie Rhodes for typing the manuscript and to the following for critically reading the manuscript: Linda Buckner (Coe), Barbara Edelberg, Martin W. Ham, Robert Malow, Priscilla Richardson, Donald Scott, Elaine Waters, and Sheryl Wilson.

References

Abelson, P.H. Editorial. *Science*, Oct. 12, 1962.

Adair, J.G., and Epstein, J.S. Verbal cues in the mediation of experimenter bias. *Psychological Reports*, 1968, 22, 1045-1053.

Adair, J.G. *The Human Subject: The Social Psychology of the Psychological Experiment.* Boston: Little, Brown, 1973.

Adler, N.E. Impact of prior sets given experimenters and subjects on the experimenter expectancy effect. *Sociometry*, 1973, 36, 113-126.

Andreski, S. *Social Science as Sorcery*, London: Andre Deutsch, 1972.

Anonymous. A record of success. *Pensée*, 1972, 2(no. 2), 11-15, 23. (a)

Anonymous. Seeing over the proton. *Science News*, July 8, 1972, 102, 20-21. (b)

Anonymous. *Publication Manual of the American Psychological Association.* (2nd Ed.) Washington, D.C.: American Psychological Association, 1974.

Argyris, C. Diagnosing defenses against the outsider. *Journal of Social Issue*, 1952, 8, 24-34.

Argyris, C. Some unintended consequences of rigorous research. *Psychological Bulletin*, 1968, 70, 185-197.

Ary, D., Jacobs, L.C., and Asghar, R. *Introduction to Research in Education.* New York: Holt, Rinehart, and Winston, 1972.

Azrin, N.H., Holz, W., Ulrich, R., and Goldiamond, I. The control of the content of conversation through reinforcement. *Journal of the Experimental Analysis of Behavior*, 1961, 4, 25-30.

Babad, E.Y., Mann, M., and Mar-Hayim, M. Bias in scoring the WISC subtests. *Journal of Consulting and Clinical Psychology*, 1975, 43, 268.

Bakan, D. The test of significance in psychological research. In D. Bakan, *On Method.* San Francisco: Jossey-Bass, 1967. Pp. 1-29.

Barber, B. Resistance by scientists to scientific discovery. *Science*, 1961, 134, 596-602.

Barber, B., and Fox, R.C. The case of the floppy-eared rabbits: An instance of serendipity gained and serendipity lost. *American Journal of Sociology*, 1958, 64, 128-136.

Barber, B., Lally, J.J., Makarushka, J.L., and Sullivan, D. *Research on Human Subjects: Problems of Social Control in Medical Experimentation.* New York: Russell Sage Foundation, 1973.

Barber, T.X. *Hypnosis: A Scientific Approach.* New York: Van Nostrand Reinhold, 1969. (a)

Barber, T.X. Invalid arguments, postmortem analyses, and the experimenter bias effect. *Journal of Consulting and Clinical Psychology*, 1969, 33, 11-14. (b)

Barber, T.X. *LSD, Marihuana, Yoga, and Hypnosis.* Chicago: Aldine, 1970. (a)

Barber, T.X. *Suggested ('Hypnotic') Behavior: The Trance Paradigm versus an Alternative Paradigm.* Medfield, Mass.: Medfield Foundation, 1970. (b)

Barber, T.X., Calverley, D.S., Forgione, A., McPeake, J.D., Chaves, J.F., and Bowen, B. Five attempts to replicate the experimenter bias effect. *Journal of Consulting and Clinical Psychology*, 1969, 33, 1-6.

Barber, T.X., and Silver, M.J. Fact, fiction, and the experimenter bias effect. *Psychological Bulletin* (Monograph Supplement), 1968, 70 (No. 6, Pt. 2), 1-29. (a).

Barber, T.X., and Silver, M.J. Pitfalls in data analysis and interpretation: A reply to Rosenthal. *Psychological Bulletin* (Monograph Supplement), 1968, 70, (No. 6, Pt. 2), 48-62. (b)

Barber, T.X., Spanos, N.P., and Chaves, J.F. *Hypnosis, Imagination, and Human Potentialities.* Elmsford, N.Y.: Pergamon Press, 1974.

Bargmann, V., and Motz, L. On the discoveries concerning Jupiter and Venus, *Science*, 1962, 138, 1350-1352.

Barko, G.D. Experimenter bias effect as a function of ambiguity. Doctoral dissertation, University of North Dakota, 1970. Ann

Arbor, Mich.: University Microfilms, No. 71-15, 649.

Bauernfeind, R.H. The need for replication in education research. *Phi Delta Kappan*, 1968, 50, 126-128.

Beasley, D.S., and Manning, J.I. Experimenter bias and speech pathologists' evaluation of children's language skills. *Journal of Communication Disorders*, 1973, 6, 93-101.

Beck, W.S. *Modern Science and the Nature of Life.* Garden City, N.Y.: Doubleday, 1961.

Becker, H.G. Experimenter expectancy, experience and status as factors in observational data. Master's thesis, University of Saskatchewan, 1968.

Bell, R.R. Experimenter expectancy in pupillometric research. *Perceptual and Motor Skills*, 1971, 33, 174.

Benney, M., Riesman, D., and Star, Shirley, A. Age and sex in the interview. *American Journal of Sociology*, 1956, 62, 143-152.

Berkowitz, L. Reporting an experiment: A case study in leveling, sharpening, and assimilation. *Journal of Experimental Social Psychology*, 1971, 7, 237-243.

Binder, A., McConnell, D., and Sjoholm, Nancy A. Verbal conditioning as a function of experimenter characteristics. *Journal of Abnormal and Social Psychology*, 1957, 55, 309-314.

Blake, B.F., and Heslin, R. Evaluation apprehension and subject bias in experiments. *Journal of Experimental Research in Personality*, 1971, 5, 57-63.

Blanchard, E.B. A comparison of reciprocal inhibition and reactive inhibition therapies in the treatment of anxiety: A methodological critique. *Behavioral Therapy*, 1971, 2, 103-106.

Blatchley, R.J. Examiner and subject expectancy effects on the WAIS. Master's thesis, Loyola College, 1970.

Bloom, R., and Tesser, A. On reducing experimenter bias: The effects of forewarning. *Canadian Journal of Behavioral Science*, 1971, 3, 198-208.

Boalt, G. *The Sociology of Research.* Carbondale, Ill.: Southern Illinois University Press, 1969.

Bootzin, R.R. Expectancy and individual differences in experimenter bias. *Journal of General Psychology*, 1971, 84, 303-312.

Borg, W.R., and Gall, M.C. *Educational Research: An Introduction.* (2nd Ed.) New York: David McKay, 1971.

Bozarth, J.D., and Roberts, R.R., Jr. Signifying significant significance. *American Psychologist*, 1972, 27, 774-775.

Brush, S.G. Should history of science be rated X? *Science*, 1974, 183, 1164-1172.

Cannell, C.F., and Kahn, R.L. Interviewing. In G. Lindzey, & E. Aronson (Eds.) *The Handbook of Social Psychology*. Vol. II (2nd ed.) Reading, Mass.: Addison-Wesley, 1968. Pp. 526-595.

Carlson, R. Where is the person in personality research? *Psychological Bulletin*, 1971, 75, 203-219.

Cattell, R.B. (Ed.) *Handbook of Multivariate Experimental Psychology*. Chicago: Rand McNally, 1966.

Chapanis, A. Engineering psychology. *Annual Review of Psychology*, 1963, 14, 285-318.

Chapanis, N.P., and Chapanis, A. Cognitive dissonance: Five years later. *Psychological Bulletin*, 1964, 61, 1-22.

Chaves, J.F. Hypnosis reconceptualized: An overview of Barber's theoretical and empirical work. *Psychological Reports*, 1968, 22, 587-608.

Clement, D.E. Quasi-sensory communication: Still not proved. *Journal of Personality and Social Psychology*, 1972, 23, 103-104.

Cohen, J. The statistical power of abnormal-social psychological research: A review. *Journal of Abnormal and Social Psychology*, 1962, 65, 145-153.

Cohen, J. Some statistical issues in psychological research. In B.B. Wolman (Ed.) *Handbook of Clinical Psychology*. New York: McGraw-Hill, 1965. Chap. 5.

Compton, J.W. Experimenter bias: Reaction time and types of expectancy information. *Perceptual and Motor Skills*, 1970, 31, 159-168.

Cooper, E.S. Direct observation? *Bulletin of the British Psychological Society*, 1974, 27, 3-7.

Cordaro, L., and Ison, J.R. Observer bias in classical conditioning of the planarian. *Psychological Reports*, 1963, 13, 787-789.

Craig, J.R., and Reese, S.C. Retention of raw data: A Problem revisited. *American Psychologist*, 1973, 28, 723.

Crane, D.M. The environment of discovery. Doctoral dissertation, Columbia University, 1964.

Crane, D. The gatekeepers of science: Some factors affecting the selection of articles for scientific journals. *American Sociologist*, 1967, 2, 195-201.

Culliton, B.J. The Sloan-Kettering affair (II): An uneasy resolution. *Science*, 1974, 184, 1154-1157.

Dana, J.M., and Dana, R.H. Experimenter-bias and the WAIS. *Perceptual and Motor Skills*, 1969, 28, 694.

Dangel, H.L. The biasing effect of pretest information on the WISC scores of mentally retarded children. Doctoral dissertation,

Pennsylvania State University, 1970. Ann Arbor, Mich.: University Microfilms, Order No. 71-16, 588.

Dangel, H.L. Biasing effect of pretest referral information on WISC scores of mentally retarded children. *American Journal of Mental Deficiency*, 1972, 77, 354-359.

de Grazia, A. The scientific reception system. In A. de Grazia, R.E. Juergens, and L.C. Stecchini (Eds.). *The Velikovsky Affair: Scientism vs. Science*. New Hyde Park, N.Y.: University Books, 1966, Pp. 171-231.

de Grazia, A., Juergens, R.E., and Stecchini, L.D. *The Velikovsky Affair: Scientism versus Science*. New Hyde Park, N.Y.: University Books, 1966.

Denzin, N.K. *The Research Act: A Theoretical Introduction to Sociological Methods*. Chicago: Aldine, 1970.

de Solla Price. *Science Since Babylon*. New Haven: Yale University Press, 1961.

Dickstein, L.S., and Kephart, J.L. Effect of explicit examiner expectancy upon WAIS performance, *Psychological Reports*, 1972, 30, 207-212.

Duggan, T.J., and Dean, C.W. Common misinterpretations of significance levels in sociological journals. *American Sociologist*, 1968, 3, 45-46.

Duncan, S.D., Jr., Rosenberg, M.J., and Finkelstein, J. The paralanguage of experimenter bias. *Sociometry*, 1969, 32, 207-219.

Duncan, S., and Rosenthal, R. Vocal emphasis in experimenters' instruction reading as unintended determinant of subjects' responses. *Language and Speech*, 1968, 11, 20-26.

Dunnette, M.D. Fads, fashions, and folderol in psychology. *American Psychologist*, 1966, 21, 343-352.

Dunnette, M.D., and Heneman, H. Influence of scale administrator on employee attitude responses. *Journal of Applied Psychology*, 1956, 40, 73-77.

Dusek, J.B. Experimenter bias in performance of children at a simple motor task. *Developmental Psychology*, 1971, 4, 55-62.

Dusek, J.B. Experimenter-bias effects on the simple motor task performance of low- and high-test anxious boys and girls. *Psychological Reports*, 1972, 30, 107-114.

DuShane, G., Krauskopf, K.B., Lerner, E.M., Morse, P.M., Steinbach, H.B., Strauss, W.L., Jr., and Tatum, E.L. An unfortunate event. *Science*, 1961, 134, 945-946.

Edgington, E.J. Contradictory conclusions from two speed of performance measures. *Psychological Bulletin*, 1960, 57, 315-317.

Egeland, B. Examiner expectancy: Effects on the scoring of the WISC. *Psychology in the Schools*, 1969, 6, 313-315.

Elashoff, J.D., and Snow, R.E. *Pygmalion reconsidered—A Case Study in Statistical Inference: Reconsideration of the Rosenthal-Jacobson Data on Teacher Expectancy.* Worthington, Ohio: Charles A. Jones Publishing Co., 1971.

Faber, B.L. The Sloan-Kettering Affair. *Science*, 1974, 185, 734.

Farrow, J.M., Farrow, B.J., Lohss, W.E., and Taub, S.I. Intersubject communication as a contaminating factor in verbal conditioning. *Perceptual and Motor Skills*, 1975, 40, 975-982.

Feild, H.S., and Armenakis, A.A. On use of multiple tests of significance in psychological research. *Psychological Reports*, 1974, 35, 427-431.

Feldman, J.J., Hyman, H., and Hart, C.W. A field study of interviewer effects on the quality of survey data. *Public Opinion Quarterly*, 1951, 15, 734-761.

Felton, G.S. Experimenter expectancy effect examined as a function of task ambiguity and internal versus external control of reinforcement. Doctoral dissertation, University of Southern California, 1970. Ann Arbor, Mich.: University Microfilms, No. 70-19, 114.

Festinger, L. Laboratory experiments. In L. Festinger and D. Katz (Eds.) *Research Methods in the Behavioral Sciences.* New York: Holt, Rinehart, and Winston, 1953.

Fleiss, J.L. Estimating the magnitude of experimental effects. *Psychological Bulletin*, 1969, 72, 273-276.

Freedman, B.E. The experimenter absent condition: A comparison with biased and unbiased experimenter effects. Master's thesis, Syracuse University, 1970.

Friedlander, F. Type I and Type II bias. *American Psychologist*, 1964, 19, 198-199.

Friedman, N. *The Social Nature of Psychological Research.* New York: Basic Books, 1967.

Fromkin, H.L., and Streufert, S. Laboratory experimentation. In M.D. Dunnette (Ed.) *The Handbook of Organizational and Industrial Psychology.* Chicago: Rand McNally, 1973.

Gallo, P.S., Jr., and Dale, I.A. Experimenter bias in the prisoner's dilemma game. *Psychonomic Science*, 1968, 13, 340.

Gillingham, W.H. An investigation of examiner influence on Wechsler Intelligence Scale for Children scores. Doctoral dissertation, Michigan State University, 1970. Ann Arbor, Mich.: University Microfilms, Order No. 70-20, 458.

Glaser, B.G. *Organizational Scientists: Their Professional Careers.* Indianapolis: Bobbs-Merrill, 1964.

Goebel, R.A., and Stewart, C.G. Effects of experimenter bias and induced subject expectancy on hypnotic susceptibility. *Journal of Personality and Social Psychology*, 1971, 18, 263-272.

Goodstein, L.D., and Brazis, K.L. Psychology of the scientist: XXX. Credibility of psychologists: An empirical study. *Psychological Reports*, 1970, 27, 835-838.

Greenwald, A.G. Consequences of prejudice against the null hypothesis. *Psychological Bulletin*, 1975, 82, 1-20.

Grice, R.G., and Hunter, J.J. Stimulus intensity effects depend upon the type of experimental design. *Psychological Review*, 1964, 71, 247-256.

Guest, L. A study of interviewer competence. *International Journal of Opinion and Attitude Research*, 1947, 1 (4), 17-30.

Guilford, J.P. *Psychometric Methods.* (2nd Ed.) New York: McGraw-Hill, 1954.

Hagstrom, W. *The Scientific Community.* New York: Basic Books, 1965.

Hansel, C.E.M. *ESP: A Scientific Evaluation.* New York: Charles Scribners, 1966.

Hansen, M.H., Hurwitz, W.N., Marks, E.S., and Mauldin, W.P. Response errors in surveys. *Journal of the American Statistical Association*, 1951, 46, 147-190.

Hanson, N.R. *The Concept of the Positron.* Cambridge: Cambridge University Press, 1963.

Harlow, H. William James and instinct theory. In R. MacCleod (Ed.) *William James: Unfinished Business.* Washington, D.C.: American Psychological Association, 1969.

Hawthorne, J.W. The influence of the set and dependence of the data collector on the experimenter bias effect. Doctoral dissertation, Duke University, 1972. Ann Arbor, Mich.: University Microfilms, Order No. 73-8081.

Hays, W.L. *Statistics for Psychologists.* New York: Holt, Rinehart, and Winston, 1963.

Hearst, E. The behavior of Skinnerians. *Contemporary Psychology*, 1967, 12, 402-404.

Hersh, J.B. Effects of referral information on testers. *Journal of Consulting and Clinical Psychology*, 1971, 37, 116-122.

Hertzog, J., and Walker, C.E. Effects of sex and need to avoid success on verbal mediation of experimenter bias. *Psychological Reports*, 1973, 32, 1235-1238.

Hipskind, N.M., and Rintelmann, W.F. Effects of experimenter bias upon pure-tone and speech audiometry. *Journal of Auditory Research*, 1969, 9, 298-305.

Hull, C.L. *Hypnosis and Suggestibility: An Experimental Approach*. New York: Appleton-Century, 1933.

Hyman, H.H. *Interviewing in Social Research*. Chicago: University of Chicago Press, 1954.

Ingraham, L.H., and Harrington, G.M. Experience of *E* as a variable in reducing experimenter bias. *Psychological Reports*, 1966, 19, 455-461.

Irving, J.J. Subjects' expectancy and need for social approval in the Rosenthal experimenter effect paradigm. Doctoral dissertation, University of Kansas, 1969. Ann Arbor, Mich.: University Microfilms, No. 69-21, 532.

Jacob, T. The experimenter bias effect: A failure to replicate. *Psychonomic Science*, 1968, 13, 239-240.

Jacob, T. The emergence and mediation of the experimenter bias effect as a function of "demand characteristics", experimenter "investment" and the nature of the experimental task. Doctoral dissertation, the University of Nebraska. Ann Arbor, Mich.: University Microfilms, 1970, No. 69-22, 279.

Jacob, T. Experimenter bias effect as a function of demand characteristics and experimenter investment. *Psychological Reports*, 1971, 28, 1003-1010.

Janssen, J.P. The experimenter's expectation-effect: An artifact of non-standardized experimental conditions? An investigation concerning Rosenthal's experimenter-bias under standardized group experimental conditions. [Germ] *Psychologische Beiträge*, 1973, 15, 230-248.

Jastrow, J. *Errors and Eccentricity in Human Belief*. New York: Dover, 1935.

Johnson, R.F.Q. The experimenter attributes effect: A methodological analysis. *Psychological Record*, 1976, 26, 67-78.

Johnson, R.W. Subject performance as affected by experimenter expectancy, sex of experimenter, and verbal reinforcement. *Canadian Journal of Behavioral Science*, 1970, 2, 60-66.

Johnson, R.W., and Adair, J.G. The effects of systematic recording error vs. experimenter bias on latency of word association. *Journal of Experimental Research in Personality*, 1970, 4, 270-275.

Johnson, R.W., and Adair, J.G. Experimenter expectancy vs. systematic recording errors under automated and nonautomated stimulus presentation. *Journal of Experimental Research in Personality*, 1972, 6, 88-94.

Johnson, R.W., and Ryan, B.J. Observer/recorder error as affected by different tasks and different expectancy inducements. *Journal of Experimental Research in Personality*, in press.

Johnson, V.S. The behavior therapy controversy: A study on observer bias, reliability, and information. Doctoral dissertation, Iowa State University, 1970. Ann Arbor, Mich.: University Microfilms, Order No. 71-7285.

Jones, R.A., and Cooper, J. Mediation of experimenter effects. *Journal of Personality and Social Psychology*, 1971, 20, 70-74.

Jung, J. *The Experimenter's Dilemma*. New York: Harper & Row, 1971.

Kamin, L.J. Heredity, intelligence, politics, and psychology. Paper presented at Eastern Psychological Association annual meeting, Washington, D.C., May 5, 1973.

Katahn, M., and Koplin, J.H. Paradigm clash: Comment on "Some recent criticisms of behaviorism and learning theory with special reference to Breger and McGough and to Chomsky". *Psychological Bulletin*, 1968, 69, 147-148.

Kelman, H.C. *A Time to Speak: On Human Values and Social Research*. San Francisco: Jossey-Bass, 1968.

Kennedy, J.J. Experimenter outcome bias in verbal conditioning: A failure to detect the Rosenthal effect. *Psychological Reports*, 1969, 25, 495-500.

Kennedy, J.J., Cook, P.A., and Brewer, R.R. The effects of three selected experimenter variables in verbal conditioning research. *Journal of Social Psychology*, 1970, 81, 165-175.

Kennedy, J.L. An evaluation of extra-sensory perception: *Proceedings of the American Philosophical Society*, 1952, 96, 513-518.

Kent, R.N., O'Leary, K.D., Diament, D., and Dietz, A. Expectation biases in observational evaluation of therapeutic change. *Journal of Consulting and Clinical Psychology*, 1974, 42, 774-780.

Keppel, G. *Design and Analysis: A Researcher's Handbook*. Englewood Cliffs, N.J.: Prentice-Hall, 1973.

Kerlinger, F.N. *Foundations of Behavioral Research*. New York: Holt, Rinehart and Winston, 1964.

Kessel, F.S. The philosophy of science as proclaimed and science as practiced: "Identity" or "dualism"? *American Psychologist*, 1969, 24, 999-1005.

Kessel, T., and Barber, K.J., Jr. Experimenter-subject interaction in verbal conditioning: Review of the literature. *Psychological*

Reports, 1968, 22, 59-74.

Kintz, E.L., Delprato, D.J., Mettee, D.R., Persons, C.E., and Schappe, R.H. The experimenter effect. *Psychological Bulletin*, 1965, 63, 223-232.

Kish, L. Some statistical problems in research design. In D.E. Morrison and R.E. Henkel (Eds.) *The Significance Test Controversy—A Reader.* Chicago: Aldine, 1970. Pp. 127-141.

Kish, L., and Slater, C.W. Two studies of interviewer variance of socio-psychological variables. *Proceedings of the American Statistical Association. Social Studies Section*, 1960, 66-70.

Koenigsberg, R.A. Experimenter-subject interaction in verbal conditioning. Doctoral dissertation, New School for Social Research, 1971. Ann Arbor: University Microfilms, No. 72-3729.

Koestler, A. *The Case of the Midwife Toad.* New York: Random House, 1971.

Krantz, D.L. The separate worlds of operant and non-operant psychology. *Journal of Applied Behavior Analysis*, 1971, 4, 61-70.

Kroger, R.O. The effects of role demands and test-cue properties upon personality performance. *Journal of Consulting Psychology*, 1967, 31, 304-312.

Kuhn, T.S. *The Structure of Scientific Revolution.* Chicago: University of Chicago Press, 1962.

Kuhn, T.S. Reflections on my critics. In I. Lakatos and A. Musgrave (Eds.) *Criticism and the Growth of Knowledge.* Cambridge: Cambridge University Press, 1970. Pg. 231-278.

Landon, P.B. Motivational arousal, task complexity and experimenter bias. Doctoral dissertation, Rutgers University, 1972. Ann Arbor, Mich.: University Microfilms, Order No. 72-17, 849.

Laszlo, J.P., and Rosenthal, R. Subject dogmatism, experimenter status and experimenter expectancy effects. *Personality: An International Journal*, 1971, 1, 11-23.

Levine, M. Scientific method and the adversary model: Some preliminary thoughts. *American Psychologist*, 1974, 29, 661-677.

Lipset, S.M., Trow, M.A., and Coleman, J.S. Statistical problems. In D.E. Morrison and R.E. Henkel (Eds.) *The Significance Test Controversy — A Reader.* Chicago: Aldine, 1970. Pp. 81-86.

Lykken, D.T. Statistical significance in psychological research. *Psychological Bulletin*, 1968, 70, 151-159.

MacDougall, C.D. *Hoaxes.* (2nd Ed.) New York: Ace Books, 1958.

Mahoney, M.J. Publication prejudices: Partiality toward confirming data. Dept. of Psychology, Penn. State University, 1975.

Marcia, J.E. The need for social approval, the condition of hypothesis-making, and their effects on unconscious experimenter bias. Master's thesis, Ohio State University, 1961.

Martuza, V.R. The effects of experimenter expectancy on guessing performance and level of confidence in guessing accuracy. *Psychonomic Science*, 1971, 23, 169-170.

Marwit, S.J. Communication of tester bias by means of modeling. *Journal of Projective Techniques & Personality Assessment*, 1969, 33, 345-352.

Marwit, S.J., and Marcia, J.E. Tester bias and response to projective instruments. *Journal of Consulting Psychology*, 1967, 31, 253-258.

Marwit, S.J., and Strauss, M.E. Influence of instructions on expectancy effects of Rorschach testing. *Journal of Personality Assessment*, 1975, 39, 13-18.

Masling, J. The influence of situational and interpersonal variables in projective testing. *Psychological Bulletin*, 1960, 57, 65-85.

Masling, J. Differential indoctrination of examiners and Rorschach responses. *Journal of Consulting Psychology*, 1965, 29, 198-201.

Masling, J. Role-related behavior of the subject and psychologist and its effects upon psychological data. In D. Levine (Ed.) *Nebraska Symposium on Motivation*. Lincoln, Neb.: University of Nebraska Press, 1966. Pp. 67-103.

Mayo, C. External conditions affecting experimental bias. Doctoral dissertation, University of Houston, 1972. Ann Arbor, Mich.: University Microfilms, No. 72-34, 176.

McCaa, B.B. A study of some factors mediating unintended experimenter effects upon subjects in psychological experiments. Doctoral dissertation, Washington University, 1971. Ann Arbor, Mich.: University Microfilms, Order No. 72-9355.

McCain, G., and Segal, E.M. *The Game of Science*. Belmont, Calif.: Brooks/Cole, 1969.

McFall, R.M. "Unintentional communication": The effect of congruence and incongruence between subject and experimenter construction. Doctoral dissertation, Ohio State University. Ann Arbor, Mich.: University Microfilms, 1966, Order No. 66-1809.

McFall, R.M., and Saxman, J.H. Verbal communication as a mediator of expectancy effects: Methodological artifact? *Psychological Reports*, 1968, 23, 1223-1228.

McFall, R.M., and Schenkein, D. Experimenter expectancy effects, need for achievement, and field dependence. *Journal of Experimental Research in Personality*, 1970, 4, 122-128.

McGinley, H., McGinley, P., and Murray, R. Experimenter—expectancy phenomenon: Experience of *E*, mechanical vs. manual stimulus presentation and IQ vs. success — failure judgments. *Perceptual and Motor Skills*, 1972, 34, 771-781.

McGinley, H., McGinley, P., and Shames, M. Failure to find experimenter-expectancy effects in IQ estimations. *Psychological Reports*, 1970, 27, 831-834.

McGuire, W.J. Personality and susceptibility to social influence. In E.F. Borgatta & W.W. Lambert (Eds.) *Handbook of Personality Theory and Research*. Chicago: Rand McNally, 1968. Pp. 1130-1187.

McGuire, W.J. The Yin and Yang of progress in social psychology: Seven koan. *Journal of Personality and Social Psychology*, 1973, 26, 446-456.

McNemar, Q. At random: Sense and non-sense. *American Psychologist*, 1960, 15, 295-300.

Merton, R.K. Behavior patterns of scientists. *American Scientist*, 1969, 57, 1-23.

Merton, R.K. Priorities in scientific discovery: A chapter in the sociology of science. *American Sociological Review*, 1957, 22, 635-659.

Miller, A.G. *The Social Psychology of Psychological Research*. New York: The Free Press, 1972.

Miller, K.A. A study of "experimenter bias" and "subject awareness" as demand characteristic artifacts in attitude change experiments. Doctoral dissertation, Bowling Green State University, 1970. Ann Arbor, Mich.: University Microfilms, Order No. 70-24, 955.

Miller, P.A. The effect of experimenter status and experimenter competency on the magnitude of the experimenter bias effect. Doctoral dissertation, Stanford University, 1972. Ann Arbor, Mich.: University Microfilms, Order No. 72-16, 757.

Mills, J. (Ed.) *Experimental Social Psychology*. New York: Macmillan, 1969.

Minor, M.W. Experimenter-expectancy effect as a function of evaluation apprehension. *Journal of Personality and Social Psychology*, 1970, 15, 326-332.

Minturn, E.B. A proposal of significance. *American Psychologist*, 1971, 26, 669-670.

Mitroff, I.I. Studying the lunar-rock scientist. *Saturday Review World*, Nov. 2, 1974, 64-65.

Natrella, M.G. The relation between confidence intervals and tests of significance. *American Statistician*, 1960, 14, 20-22, 33.

Neher, A. Probability pyramiding, research error and the need for independent replication. *Psychological Record*, 1967, 17, 257-262.

N.W. Physicians who falsify drug data. *Science*, 1973, 180, 1038.

Ohler, F.D. The effects of four sources of experimental bias: Evaluation apprehension, cueing, volunteer status, and choice. Doctoral dissertation, University of Southern California, 1971. Ann Arbor, Mich.: University Microfilms, Order No. 71-28, 881.

O'Leary, K.D., and Kent, R. Behavior modification for social action: Research tactics and problems. In L.A. Hamerlynck, L.C. Handy, and E.J. Mash (Eds.) *Behavior Change: Methodology, Concepts, and Practice*. Champaign, Ill.: Research Press, 1973. Pp. 69-96.

O'Leary, K.D., Kent, R.N., and Kanowitz, J. Shaping data collection congruent with experimental hypotheses. *Journal of Applied Behavioral Analysis*, 1975, 8, 43-51.

Orne, M.T. On the social psychology of the psychological experiment: With particular reference to demand characteristics and their implications. *American Psychologist*, 1962, 17, 776-783.

Orne, M.T. Demand characteristics and the concept of quasi-controls. In R. Rosenthal and R.L. Rosnow (Eds.) *Artifact in Behavioral Research*. New York: Academic Press, 1969. Pp. 143-179.

Ostrom, T.M. To replicate or explicate. *American Psychologist*, 1971, 26, 312.

Page, M.M., and Lumia, A.R. Cooperation with demand characteristics and the bimodal distribution of verbal conditioning data. *Psychonomic Science*, 1968, 12, 243-244.

Page, S. Interpersonal expectancy effects: Studies with three psychiatric samples. *Psychological Reports*, 1972, 30, 139-142.

Page, S. Social interaction and experimenter effects in the verbal conditioning experiment. *Canadian Journal of Psychology*, 1971, 25, 463-475.

Pereboom, A.C. Some fundamental problems in experimental psychology: an overview. *Psychological Reports*, 1971, 28, 439-455.

Perlmutter, L.J.P. Experimenter-subject needs for social approval and task interactiveness as factors in experimenter expectancy effects. Doctoral dissertation, Pennsylvania State University, 1971. Ann Arbor, Mich.: University Microfilms, No. 72-13, 911.

Persinger, G.W. The effect of acquaintanceship on the mediation of experimenter bias. Master's thesis, University of North Dakota, 1963.

Pflugrath, J. Examiner influence in a group testing situation with particular reference to examiner bias. Master's thesis, University of North Dakota, 1962.

Phillips, L.D. *Bayesian Statistics for Social Scientists.* New York: Crowell, 1973.

Planck, M. *Philosophy of Physics.* New York: Norton, 1936.

Platt, J.R. Strong inference. *Science,* 1964, 146, 347-353.

Plutchik, R. *Foundations of Experimental Research,* New York: Harper & Row, 1968.

Price, G.R. Science and the supernatural. *Science,* 1955, 122, 359-367.

Raffetto, A.M. Experimenter effects on subjects' reported hallucinatory experiences under visual and auditory deprivation. Master's thesis, San Francisco State College, 1967.

Raney, J.F. A plea and a plan for replication. *American Psychologist,* 1970, 25, 1176-1177.

Reif, F. The competitive world of the pure scientist. *Science,* 1961, 134, 1957-1962.

Rhine, J.B. Some avoidable heartaches in parapsychology. *Journal of Parapsychology,* 1973, 37, 355-366.

Rhine, J.B. A new case of experimenter unreliability. *Journal of Parapsychology,* 1974, 38, 215-255. (a)

Rhine, J.B. Security versus deception in parapsychology. *Journal of Parapsychology,* 1974, 38, 99-121. (b)

Roethlisberger, F.J., and Dickson, W.T. *Management and the Worker.* Cambridge, Mass.: Harvard University Press, 1946.

Rosen, N.A. Demand characteristics in a field experiment. *Journal of Applied Psychology,* 1970, 54, 163-168.

Rosen, N.A., and Sales, S.M. Behavior in a nonexperiment: The effects of behavioral field research on the work performance of factory employees. *Journal of Applied Psychology,* 1966, 50, 165-171.

Rosenthal, R. On the social psychology of the psychological experiment: The experimenter's hypothesis as unintended determinant of experimental results. *American Scientist,* 1963, 51, 268-283.

Rosenthal, R. The effect of the experimenter on the results of psychological research. In B.A. Maher (Ed.) *Progress in Experimental Personality Research.* Vol. 1. New York: Academic Press, 1964. Pp. 79-114. (a)

Rosenthal, R. Experimenter outcome-orientation and the results of the psychological experiment. *Psychological Bulletin,* 1964, 61,405-412. (b)

Rosenthal, R. *Experimenter Effects in Behavioral Research.* New York: Appleton-Century-Crofts, 1966.

Rosenthal, R. Covert communication in the psychological experiment. *Psychological Bulletin,* 1967, 67, 356-367.

Rosenthal, R. Experimenter expectancy and the reassuring nature of the null hypothesis decision procedure. *Psychological Bulletin* (Monograph Supplement), 1968, 70 (No. 6, Pt. 2), 30-47.

Rosenthal, R. Interpersonal expectations: Effects of the experimenter's hypothesis. In R. Rosenthal & R.L. Rosnow (Eds.) *Artifact in Behavioral Research.* New York: Academic Press, 1969. Pp. 181-277.

Rosenthal, R., and Fode, K.L. The effect of experimenter bias on the performance of the albino rat. *Behavioral Science,* 1963, 8, 183-189. (a)

Rosenthal, R., and Fode, K.L. Three experiments in experimenter bias. *Psychological Reports,* 1963, 12, 491-511. (b)

Rosenthal, R., Friedman, C.J., Johnson, C.A., Fode, K., Schill, T., White, R.C., and Vikan, L.L. Variables affecting experimenter bias in a group situation. *Genetic Psychology Monographs,* 1964, 70, 271-296.

Rosenthal, R., Friedman, N., and Kurland, D. Instruction-reading behavior of the experimenter as an unintended determinant of experimental results. *Journal of Experimental Research in Personality,* 1966, 1, 221-226.

Rosenthal, R., and Jacobson, L. *Pygmalion in the Classroom: Teacher Expectation and Pupils' Intellectual Development.* New York: Holt, Rinehart & Winston, 1968.

Rosenthal, R., Kohn, P., Greenfield, P.M., and Carota, N. Data desirability, experimenter expectancy, and the results of psychological research. *Journal of Personality and Social Psychology,* 1966, 3, 20-27.

Rosenthal, R., and Lawson, R. A longitudinal study of the effects of experimenter bias on the operant learning of laboratory rats. *Journal of Psychiatric Research,* 1964, 2, 61-72.

Rosenthal, R., Persinger, G.W., Mulry, R.C., Vikan-Kline, L., and Grothe, M. Changes in experimental hypotheses as determinants of experimental results. *Journal of Projective Techniques and Personality Assessment,* 1964, 28, 465-469. (a)

Rosenthal, R., Persinger, G.W., Mulry, R.C., Vikan-Kline, L., and Grothe, M. Emphasis on experimental procedure, sex of subjects, and the biasing effects of experimental hypotheses. *Journal of Projective Techniques and Personality Assessment,* 1964, 28, 470-473. (b)

Rosenthal, R., Persinger, G.W., Vikan-Kline, L., and Fode, K.L. The effect of experimenter outcome-bias and subject set on awareness in verbal conditioning experiments. *Journal of Verbal Learning and Verbal Behavior*, 1963, 2, 275-283.

Rosenthal, R., Persinger, G.W., Vikan-Kline, L., and Mulry, R.C. The role of the research assistant in the mediation of experimenter bias. *Journal of Personality*, 1963, 31, 313-335.

Rosenthal, R., and Rosnow, R.L. (Eds.) *Artifact in Behavioral Research*, New York: Academic Press, 1969.

Rosenthal, R., and Rosnow, R.L. *The Volunteer Subject.* New York: John Wiley, 1975.

Rostand, J. *Error and Deception in Science.* New York: Basic Books, 1960.

Roth, J.A. Hired hand research. *American Sociologist*, 1966, 1, 190-196.

Ryan, T.A. Multiple comparisons in psychological research. *Psychological Bulletin*, 1959, 56, 26-47.

Sarason, I.G. Individual differences, situational variables, and personality research. *Journal of Abnormal and Social Psychology*, 1962, 65, 376-380.

Sarason, I.G. Test anxiety and social influence. *Journal of Personality*, 1973, 41, 261-271.

Sarason, I.G., and Minard, J. Interrelationships among subject, experimenter, and situational variables. *Journal of Abnormal and Social Psychology*, 1963, 67, 87-91.

Sattler, J.M. *Assessment of Children's Intelligence.* Philadelphia: W.B. Saunders, 1974.

Sattler, J.M., Hillix, W.A., and Neher, L.A. Halo effect in examiner scoring of intelligence test responses. *Journal of Consulting and Clinical Psychology*, 1970, 34, 172-176.

Sattler, J.M., Skenderian, D., and Passen, A.J. Examiner's race and subjects' responses to an attitude scale. *Journal of Social Psychology*, 1972, 87, 321-322.

Saunders, B.T., and Vitro, F.T. Examiner expectancy and bias as a function of the referral process in cognitive assessment. *Psychology in the Schools*, 1971, 8, 168-171.

Scherer, K.R., Rosenthal, R., and Koivumaki, J. Mediating interpersonal expectancies via vocal cues: Differential speech intensity as a means of social influence. *European Journal of Social Psychology*, 1972, 2, 163-176.

Schroeder, H.E., and Kleinsasser, L.D. Examiner bias: A determinant of children's verbal behavior on the WISC. *Journal of Consulting and Clinical Psychology*, 1972, 39, 451-454.

Scott, W.R. Fieldwork in a formal organization: Some dilemmas in the role of observer. *Human Organization*, 1962, 22, 162-168.

Selvin, H.C. A critique of tests of significance in survey research. In D.E. Morrison and R.E. Henkel (Eds.) *The Significance Test Controversy—A Reader.* Chicago: Aldine, 1970. Pp. 94-106.

Shames, M. The ambiguity model: A dimensional analysis of experimenter expectancy effects. Doctoral dissertation, University of Manitoba, 1971.

Shames, M.L., and Adair, J.G. Experimenter-bias as a function of the type and structure of the task. Paper presented at the meeting of the Canadian Psychological Association, Ottawa, May, 1967.

Sheatsley, P.B. Some uses of interviewer-report forms. *Public Opinion Quarterly*, 1947,11, 601-611.

Sheehan, P.W. *E*-expectancy and the role of awareness in verbal conditioning. *Psychological Reports*, 1969, 24, 203-206.

Sheehan, P.W. Factors affecting mediation of *E*-bias effects in verbal operant conditioning. *Psychological Reports*, 1970, 27, 647-650.

Sherif, M. On the relevance of social psychology. *American Psychologist*, 1970, 25, 144-156.

Silver, M.J. Experimenter modeling: A critique. *Journal of Experimental Research in Personality*, 1968, 3, 172-178.

Silverman, I. The effects of experimenter outcome expectancy on latency of word association. *Journal of Clinical Psychology*, 1968, 24, 60-63.

Silverman, I. Review of R. Rosenthal and R.L. Rosnow (Eds.) *Artifact in Behavioral Research. Contemporary Psychology*, 1970, 15, 718-721.

Simon, W.E. Expectancy effects in the scoring of vocabulary items: A study of scorer bias. *Journal of Educational Measurement*, 1969, 6, 159-164.

Sjoberg, G., and Nett, R. *A Methodology for Social Research.* New York: Harper & Row, 1968.

Smart, R.G. The importance of negative results in psychological research. *Canadian Psychologist*, 1964, 5, 225-232.

Smith, R.E., and Flenning, F. Need for approval and susceptibility to unintended social influence. *Journal of Consulting and Clinical Psychology*, 1971, 36, 383-385.

Snow, C.P. The moral un-neutrality of science. *Science*, 1961, 133, 256-259.

Souren, G., van der Kloot, W., and van Bergen, A. *Het Rosenthal Effect.* Leiden, Netherlands: Psychological Institute, Rijks University, 1969.

Spanos, N.P. Barber's reconceptualization of hypnosis: An evaluation of criticisms. *Journal of Experimental Research in Personality*, 1970, 4, 241-258.

Spanos, N.P., and Chaves, J.F. Hypnosis research: A methodological critique of experiments generated by two alternative paradigms. *American Journal of Clinical Hypnosis*, 1970, 13, 108-127.

Steinhelber, J.C. Bias in the assessment of psychotherapy. *Journal of Consulting and Clinical Psychology*, 1970, 34, 37-42.

Sterling, T.D. Publication decisions and their possible effects on inferences drawn from tests of significance—or vice versa. *Journal of the American Statistical Association*, 1959, 54, 30-34.

Stevenson, H.W., and Allen, S. Adult performance as a function of sex of experimenter and sex of subject. *Journal of Abnormal and Social Psychology*, 1964, 68, 214-216.

Stove, D. The scientific Mafia. *Pensee*, 1972, 2, (No. 2), 6-8, 49.

Strauss, M.E. Examiner expectancy: Effects on Rorschach experience balance. *Journal of Consulting and Clinical Psychology*, 1968, 32, 125-129.

Strauss, M.E., and Marwit, S.J. Expectancy effects in Rorschach testing. *Journal of Consulting and Clinical Psychology*, 1970, 34, 448.

Sudman, S., and Bradburn, W.M. *Response Effects in Surveys.* Chicago: Aldine, 1974.

Summers, G.F., and Hammonds, A.D. Toward a paradigm of respondent bias in survey research. U. Wisconsin, 1965: (Cited by Rosenthal in *Experimenter Effects in Behavioral Research.* New York: Appleton-Century-Crofts, 1966).

Taylor, A. Meaning and matter. In C. Muses and A.M. Young (Eds.) *Consciousness and Reality.* New York: Outerbridge & Lazard, 1972. Pp. 165-178.

Thalhofer, N.N. Experimenter bias in reporting opinion statements. *Psychological Reports*, 1969, 24, 470.

Thompson, E.N. A Plea for replication. *California Journal of Educational Research*, 1974, 25, 79-86.

Timaeus, E., and Lueck, H.E. Experimenter expectancy and social facilitation: I. Aggression under coaction. *Psychological Reports*, 1968, 23, 456-458.(a).

Timaeus, E., and Lueck, H.E. Experimenter expectancy and social facilitation: II. Stroop-test performance under the condition of audience. *Perceptual and Motor Skills*, 1968, 27, 492-494.(b)

Tinstman, S.O. Experimenter bias and the effects of psychotherapy. Doctoral dissertation, University of Oklahoma, 1970. Ann Arbor,

Mich.: University Microfilms, Order No. 70-16, 847.

Tittle, C.R., and Rowe, A.R. Moral appeal, sanction threat, and deviance: An experimental test. *Social Problems*, 1973, 20, 488-498.

Todd, J.L. Social evaluation orientation, task orientation, and deliberate cueing in experimenter bias effect. Doctoral dissertation, University of California, L.A., 1971. Ann Arbor, Mich.: University Microfilms, No. 71-19, 462.

Toulmin, S. Does the distinction between normal and revolutionary science hold water? In I. Lakatos and A. Musgrave (Eds.) *Criticism and the Growth of Knowledge.* Cambridge: Cambridge University Press, 1970. Pp. 39-47.

Tullock, G. *The Organization of Inquiry.* Durham, N.C.: Duke University Press, 1966.

Uno, Y. Unintended experimenter behavior as determinant of experimental results among Japanese experimenters and subjects. *Psychologia*, 1974, 17, 140-149.

Uno, Y., Frager, R.D., Takashima, K., Scherer, K.R., and Rosenthal, R. Interpersonal expectancy effects among Japanese experimenters and subjects. *Psychologia*, 1970, 13, 130-134.

Walters, C., Shurley, J.T., and Parsons, O.A. Differences in male and female responses to underwater sensory deprivation: An exploratory study. *Journal of Nervous and Mental Disease*, 1962, 135, 302-310.

Wartenberg-Ekren, R. The effects of experimenter knowledge of a subject's scholastic standing on the performance of a reasoning task. Master's thesis, Marquette University, 1962.

Watkins, J. Against normal science. In I. Lakatos and A. Musgrave (Eds.) *Criticism and the Growth of Knowledge.* Cambridge: Cambridge University Press, 1970. Pp. 25-37.

Watson, J.D. *The Double Helix.* New York: Atheneum, 1968.

Weber, S.J., and Cook, T.D. Subject effects in laboratory research: An examination of subject roles, demand characteristics, and valid inference. *Psychological Bulletin*, 1972, 77, 273-295.

Weiss, L.R. The effect of subject, experimenter, and task variables on subject compliance with the experimenter's expectation. Doctoral Dissertation, State University of New York at Buffalo, 1969. Ann Arbor, Mich.: University Microfilms, Order No. 69-20, 594.

Wessler, R.L. Experimenter expectancy effects in psychomotor performance. *Perceptual and Motor Skills*, 1968, 26, 911-917.

Wessler, R.L. Experimenter expectancy effects in three dissimilar tasks. *Journal of Psychology*, 1969, 71, 63-67.

Wessler, R.L., and Strauss, M.E. Experimenter expectancy: A failure to replicate. *Psychological Reports*, 1968, 22, 687-688.

Westfall, R.S. Newton and the fudge factor. *Science*, 1973, 179, 751-758.

White, C.R. The effect of induced subject expectations on the experimenter bias situation. Unpublished doctoral dissertation, University of North Dakota, 1962.

White, J.G., Hegarty, J.R., and Beasley, N.A. Eye contact and observer bias: A research note. *British Journal of Psychology*, 1970, 61, 271-273.

Winkel, G.H., and Sarason, I.G. Subject, experimenter, and situational variables in research on anxiety. *Journal of Abnormal and Social Psychology*, 1964, 68, 601-608.

Wolins, L. Responsibility for raw data. *American Psychologist*, 1962, 17, 657-658.

Wood, R.W. The *n* - rays. *Nature*, 1904, 70, 530-531.

Wuebben, P.L., Straits, B.C., and Schulman, G.I. *The Experiment as a Social Occasion*. Berkeley, Calif.: Glendessary Press, 1974.

Wyatt, D.F., and Campbell, D.T. A study of interviewer bias as related to interviewers' expectations and own opinions. *International Journal of Opinion and Attitude Research*, 1950, 4, 77-83.

Yagoda, G., and Wolfson, W. Examiner influence on projective test responses. *Journal of Clinical Psychology*, 1964, 20, 389.

Yarom, N. Temporal localization and communication of experimenter expectancy effect with 10-11 year old children. Doctoral dissertation, University of Illinois, 1971. Ann Arbor, Mich.: University Microfilms, No. 71-21, 264.

Yarrow, M.R., Campbell, J.D., and Burton, R.V. *Child Rearing: An Inquiry into Research and Methods*. San Francisco: Jossey-Bass, 1968.

Zegers, R.A. Expectancy and the effects of confirmation and disconfirmation. *Journal of Personality and Social Psychology*, 1968, 9, 67-71.

Ziman, J.M. *Public Knowledge: An Essay Concerning the Social Dimension of Science*. Cambridge: Cambridge University Press, 1968.

Zobel, E.J., and Lehman, R.S. Interaction of subject and experimenter expectancy effects in a tone length discrimination task. *Behavioral Science*, 1969, 14, 357-363.

Name Index

Subject Index

TITLES IN THE PERGAMON GENERAL PSYCHOLOGY SERIES (Continued)